W9-AQN-860

THE RIGHTS OF PARENTS

The National Committee for Citizens in Education is happy to record special appreciation to The New World Foundation for its financial support and for expressions of encouragement in seeing this effort through to completion.

THE RIGHTS OF PARENTS

In The Education Of Their Children

David Schimmel
Louis Fischer

Published by

The National Committee for Citizens in Education
Suite 410, Wilde Lake Village Green
Columbia, Maryland 21044

First Printing
November 1977
Second Printing
June 1978

Library of Congress Catalog Card Number 77-90016

MANUFACTURED AND PRINTED IN THE
UNITED STATES OF AMERICA

Dedication

For our children:

Josie, Jonathan, and Suzanne;

Judy, Cathy, and Valerie.

And all other children—

the ultimate beneficiaries

of parents' rights.

About the Authors:

David Schimmel and *Louis Fischer* are both lawyers and Professors of Education at the University of Massachusetts, Amherst. They are coauthors of *The Civil Rights of Teachers* (Harper & Row, 1973) and *The Civil Rights of Students* (Harper & Row, 1975) and have published numerous articles on law and on education.

Acknowledgements

We wish to acknowledge and thank those who helped us in this effort: Katharine Auchincloss, Chrissie Bamber, Mike Goodman, Jenny Johnson, Crystal Kuykendall, Carl Marburger, Chris McGough and Stan Salett for their helpful criticism; David Hackett and Bunny Roncezik for special help; Mitchell Rogovin, Paul Tractenberg and Paul Weckstein for sharing their legal perspectives; Stuart Sandow for linking us with this project; Nancy Gross for her excellent editing; Bill Rioux for his leadership in coordinating the editing and publication; and the Governing Board of the National Committee for Citizens in Education for encouraging and supporting this venture.

Preface

The time has come to tell all parents that a respectable foundation of legal rights exists in this country for school children and their parents. It has taken authors Schimmel and Fischer and the National Committee for Citizens in Education to identify and catalogue these rights in a way that parents and school officials can readily understand. Directed primarily at parents and other interested citizens, this book clears away a tangle of legal technicalities that manage to obscure basic legal principles. The description of court-tested, common law and statutory rights which parents and school children now possess offers good news to parents and should stimulate them to exercise their rights under the law.

Parents are natural advocates for their children. But in school situations the authority of parents to act on behalf of their children's interest is often challenged, sometimes unreasonably. Without a working knowledge of the law, parents are at a disadvantage when it comes to pressing for their children's rights in school. Mothers and fathers are frequently held back by past experiences with laws and school policies that possess the strength of laws—and laws which have had the effect of limiting the rights of parents rather than extending or safeguarding them. In the past, lengthy and costly court suits seemed the only procedure for demanding fair treatment. Yet lawsuits are a serious step for most families and the worry of possible harm done to children by the legal process may be greater than any possible gains made by winning the case.

I am hopeful that with the availability of this kind of book we are entering a better time, a time when parents and educators who understand the law and its possibilities and limitations begin to form partnerships. This kind of cooperation between informed parents and school people could go a long way toward ending unproductive challenges, anger, expensive legal actions and attitudes which are not in the best interests of children. If this book helps set that course, it will have made an important contribution to all our lives. I encourage you to read it and use it as a reference during your children's school years.

ROBERT COLES
Harvard University
October, 1977

Contents

The primary role of the parents in the upbringing of their children is now established beyond debate as an enduring American tradition.

The U.S. Supreme Court
Wisconsin v. Yoder (1972)

Chapter 1
Overview

This book is about the legal rights that parents have in the education of their children, from kindergarten through high school. These rights are of two kinds, both equally important: the rights that parents have on their own, as parents, and the rights they have as agents for their children, who also have legal rights as students. The first kind was established by the Supreme Court in 1924 when it ruled that parents have the right to direct the education of their children,[1]* and the second in 1975 when it ruled that students "do not shed their rights at the schoolhouse door." [3]** This means that now almost all the constitutional rights that apply to adults in the community also apply to young people in the public schools.

What are these rights? In brief, they are:

> the right to a free education, the right to be protected against harm, the right to inspect student records, the right to special education for students with special needs, the right to due process of law, the right to equal educational opportunity, the right to freedom from unreasonable search and seizure, the right to freedom of expression, and the right to freedom of religion and conscience.

All these rights have now been established by law. But none of them will have any practical significance unless you, as parents, know about them and are willing to do what is necessary to see that they are carried out.

But it is not the purpose of this book to encourage you to go to court. On the contrary, its goal is to help resolve educational conflicts without going to lawyers or resorting to the courts. How? By helping parents to become legally literate—by informing them about their rights, about the way the

---

[1] Numbered footnotes refer to publications and to court cases. These have been grouped together at the back of the book.

* This right was reaffirmed in 1972, when the Court ruled that parents have the right "to guide the education of their children." [2]

** This decision expanded a Supreme Court ruling of 1969, which held that students do not shed their rights "to freedom of speech or expression at the schoolhouse gate." [4]

legal system works, and about the way it can work for them in the public schools. With this kind of information, parents will be able to practice "preventive law." This does not mean they will be able to be their own lawyers, but that they will know when the rights of their children are violated and will also know how to protect their children within the educational system.

Why will you be able to protect your and your children's rights without going to court? Because although some administrators may deliberately break the law, most unlawful school practices are the result of legal ignorance or misunderstanding, and because most administrators are anxious to avoid lawsuits—especially those they would probably lose. Where parents are able to show that school policies are unlawful, administrators would rather change them voluntarily than as a result of a court order.

Why are many educators so poorly informed about the rights of parents and students? Because most of these rights did not exist when the educators were students and because they learned almost nothing about this subject during their educations. As a result, they have had little training in applying these rights in their schools, and very little has been written that could assist them. It is our hope that this volume will help fill the gap—for educators, as well as for parents.

In addition, our book will try to demystify the law for parents—to break through the barrier of professional jargon and legalese that lawyers use among themselves by translating that legalese into English.

In short, the purpose of this book is to enable parents of public school students to constructively take the law into their own hands—to provide them with the knowledge necessary to assert their rights and to bring violations to the attention of teachers, administrators and other parents so that they can help their children receive the kind of education to which they are legally entitled.

The rights that parents have spring from three main sources: (*1*) the federal and state constitutions; (*2*) the legal tradition called the common law, as it is reflected in the decisions of our courts; (*3*) statutes and regulations of the federal and state governments, and local school board policies.

The United States Constitution is the basic law of the land, and when it is interpreted by the Supreme Court, the interpretation is binding on all state and federal courts. Moreover, since 1975, when the Supreme Court ruled that school officials could be held personally liable for damages if they violated a student's clearly established constitutional rights,[5] teachers and administrators have become more conscious of the constitutional rights of children and more responsive to legitimate complaints that are based on these rights. Chapters *2* through *7* of this book focus on rights that derive from the U.S. Constitution, as established by the Supreme Court and other federal courts.

Chapter *2* is about a student's right to be treated fairly by a school disciplinary system. It covers the procedural protections required by the Constitution before a public school can suspend or expel a student or search his locker and discusses the question of whether corporal punishment violates a student's constitutional rights.

Chapter *3* deals with the First Amendment protections of freedom of speech and press. It considers the extent and limits of a student's right to say and print whatever she * wishes—in the classroom and on the campus, in underground papers and in school publications.

Chapter *4* deals with freedom of religion and the separation of church and state as it affects the public schools, examining such issues as prayer in the classroom, state aid to parochial schools, and whether parents may disregard compulsory attendance laws for religious reasons.

Chapter *5* is about personal appearance. It considers whether students have a constitutional right to wear the hairstyle and clothing of their choice and when schools have the right to restrict dress and grooming.

Chapters *6* and *7* focus on the constitutional right of equal educational opportunity and the violation of this right because of racial or sexual discrimination. It examines such controversial issues as busing to achieve desegregation and whether all school athletic teams should be open equally to boys and girls.

Chapters *8* to *10* focus on the common law and state control of education. The common law, with its origin in English law that predates the Constitution, is the oldest source of parental rights. These chapters deal with state laws, regulations and court decisions concerning student injuries and the balance between parental and state control over education. The laws and regulations in this area vary considerably from state to state.

---

* Although it is customary to use the pronoun "he" to refer to the third person singular, we prefer to alternate "she" and "he" throughout the book, except where individuals are specifically identified.

Chapter *8* deals with the rights of parents to recover compensation when their children are injured and indicates what parents have to prove to hold schools liable for negligence.

Chapter *9* considers whether parents can collect damages from schools for poor teaching and discusses other methods of holding schools accountable. It also examines the extent to which concerned parents can influence the school curriculum in such areas as sex education, religious values, and the use of vulgar language.

Chapter *10* deals with conflicts between individual parents who wish to control the schooling of their own children and the responsibility of the state to educate all children. It considers such issues as the right of parents to educate their children at home or to withdraw them from objectionable classes or dangerous schools.

Federal statutory rights are the subject of chapters *11* and *12*. Education has traditionally been a state function, and hundreds of statutes in different states provide parents with specific rights in the education of their children. (In 1974, the Lawyers Committee for Civil Rights Under Law published a detailed report on legal standards of the 50 states for the provision of public education.[6]) Since these provisions are so diverse, we focus on parental rights that are based on powerful federal statutes enacted by Congress during recent years. Although federal legislation in education is not comprehensive, many of its provisions are far reaching and may be a model for parental involvement in the education of their children. A new law concerning handicapped children, for example, gives parents the right to be involved in the development of individualized educational plans for their own handicapped youngsters; it also guarantees their right to object to a plan they believe is unsatisfactory and to seek one they think meets their child's special needs. Many parents believe these rights would be useful in the education of every child.

Chapter *11* is about the rights of parents in connection with their children's school records. It outlines the major provisions of the Family Educational Rights and Privacy Act of 1974, which limits access to student records by outsiders, guarantees access to parents, and provides procedures for parents to challenge and correct false or misleading information contained in the records.

Chapter *12* discusses the new federal law mentioned above, which covers the rights of parents of children with special educational needs. It focuses on the Education for All Handicapped Children's Act of 1975 and explains its broad provisions, which spell out the rights of parents and students for whom special individualized education is now mandated.

Chapter *13* confronts several other topics related to parents' rights. It considers two federal statutes which provide special rights to poor parents and their children and to parents and children who do not speak English. It also considers such issues as the meaning of a "free" public education; the financing of public schools; the openness of school board meetings; the use of school facilities by parent groups; and tracking and testing.

Our final chapter is about legal literacy for parents: it discusses ways parents can learn more about the law and ways that legal literacy can be improved throughout the country.

Each chapter begins with an introduction which describes the issues or topics to be examined. Most chapters then present and examine a few important judicial decisions that outline the major legal principles involved, describing the court's reasoning in reaching its decision. This is usually followed by a series of questions and answers about issues of interest to parents. Each chapter ends by summarizing the law on the subject.

While the chapters are designed to be read in sequence, we have tried to write each one so that it can be understood if read alone. The choice is yours—whether to read the book straight through or to skip among the chapters that interest you. Although most constitutional rights and education laws are mainly applicable to public schools, we hope the book will also be useful to parents of private school students who want to encourage these schools to shape their policies according to constitutional standards.*

The appendix includes the Constitutional amendments most relevant to the rights of parents and their children. It also includes excerpts from landmark Supreme Court cases and selections from a few federal statutes and regulations of particular significance to parents. In addition, it explains how you can look up the full text of the cases cited in the book. Although we do not always agree with the decisions we discuss, we try to present an objective picture of what the law is rather than our personal views of what it ought to be.

This short volume cannot address all major conflicts involving parents

---

* Contract law and some due process principles apply to private schools, but generally the Bill of Rights prohibits only *public* officials from interfering with individual freedom.

and education. It does not, for example, explore the difficulties that arise when parents and their children disagree about student rights and educational goals. Nor does it examine ways to resolve disagreements among competing groups of parents who hold reasonable, sincere and strong opposing views.

The law examined in this book is neither simple nor unchanging. Many of the cases are as difficult to resolve for lawyers and judges as they are for parents and educators. This is because they do not involve simple conflicts of right against wrong, but complex issues of rights in conflict. And when the constitutional rights of parents and educators collide, the job of the courts is not to choose one over the other but to try to balance and protect both. Moreover, education law is constantly changing. New legislation is passed, regulations are changed, school boards revise their policies, and the Supreme Court may reverse the decision of a lower court.

Because of this diversity and change, our discussion of the cases and laws in each chapter is intended to be illustrative, not exhaustive. We have chosen to highlight major cases and legislation of general interest to parents rather than to focus on legal details.

To summarize, this book is an introduction to legal literacy for parents. It examines a wide range of constitutional, statutory, and common law rights that parents can assert on behalf of their children and their children's education. Since no two cases are exactly alike, and since the law is constantly changing, the book cannot be a substitute for legal advice.

If for any reason you contemplate legal action, you should first consult with a knowledgeable lawyer or a legal services office. But since the judicial resolution of an educational dispute is often an unhappy, expensive, difficult, and time-consuming process, bringing suit should be a last resort. Parents and educators usually share many goals. If this book does its job properly, it should help you resolve disputes through mutual education, discussion, and negotiation.

Chapter 2
Discipline and Due Process

In simple English, procedural due process basically means fair procedure. It is now the law that schools should use fair procedures with students and their parents in all matters. Whether your child is on the carpet for violating a school dress-code, for disturbing classes by handing out supposedly obscene newspapers, for starting fights in the cafeteria, or for any other reason, fair procedures (due process) should be used to determine his guilt or innocence. Thus, due process applies to all the chapters in this book. In this chapter, however, we focus specifically on the relationship between due process and discipline, in connection with such questions as the following:

- Must due process be used before your child is suspended from school? Does it make a difference if it is a short suspension, a long one or an expulsion?
- Are schools becoming more like courts than educational institutions?
- Do parents have the right to use a lawyer in school disciplinary procedures?
- May schools use corporal punishment?
- May school officials search your child and his locker?
- May students be punished for breaking rules they didn't know about or for out-of-school behavior?
- May grades be lowered for improper conduct? May diplomas be withheld for misbehavior?

Among the many disciplinary techniques schools use, suspension is one of the most frequent. It is a way of protecting other students from the suspended student's disrupting influence. The technique also involves the parents, since they are usually notified of the suspension and often must talk with officials before their child is readmitted.

In the past, school officials could suspend students for several days without elaborate proceedings. In recent years, however, this power has been challenged by students and parents. The Supreme Court faced the question in *Goss* v. *Lopez*,[1] which is discussed below.

Must due process be used before your child is suspended from school?

Nine high school students were suspended without a hearing for up to 10 days each by the Columbus, Ohio, Board of Education in 1971. Some were suspended for disruptive or disobedient conduct, some "for demonstrating in the school auditorium while a class was being conducted there," others for physically attacking police officers who were in the school to help control demonstrations, and still others for "disturbance in the lunchroom which involved some physical damage to school property."

An Ohio law gave the officials the right to suspend students without a hearing for up to 10 days provided that parents were notified of the suspension within 24 hours and given the reasons for it. The students and their parents claimed the law was unconstitutional, and the Supreme Court agreed with them.

In a 5 to 4 decision, the Court held that once a state provides public schools for its children, the students have a *property right* in attending them and that this property right may not be taken away without at least some minimal fair procedures. Furthermore, held the Court, suspension or expulsion damages a student's reputation. And since "the Due Process clause also forbids arbitrary deprivation of liberty 'Where a person's good name, reputation, honor, or integrity is at stake because of what the government is doing to him,' the minimal requirements of the clause must be satisfied." Thus the Court found that the students' liberty as well as their property rights were violated by the denial of fair procedures.

School officials argued that a short term suspension is a trivial matter that does not merit constitutional protection. But the Court disagreed. Asserting that "education is perhaps the most important function of state and local governments," the Court ruled that although some suspensions might be trivial, the power to suspend for up to 10 days is certainly important to the student and cannot be exercised arbitrarily.

Does it make a difference how long the suspension is?

The justices were well aware of the complexities of our schools and of the need for order and discipline. They recognized that school officials need the power of suspension, but they saw no reason such power could not be exercised fairly. As a minimum, they ruled, fairness would require an informal notice and a hearing. This means that the student should be told of the charges against him, orally or in writing, and if he denies them, must be given "an explanation of the evidence the authorities have and an opportunity to present his side of the story." This procedure can be carried out quite informally; as the court pointed out, good teachers and administrators have followed such fair procedures for a long time, without being forced by the law. Similarly, parents who are not arbitrary in disciplining their children give them a fair chance to present their side of the story.

Some emergencies can occur at school in which prior notice and hearing are not necessary—when, for example, there is danger to persons or property. In such cases the Court requires only that fair procedures be followed as soon as practicable after the danger has been removed. Otherwise, an informal notice and hearing should be provided for any suspension, and the longer the probable suspension the more careful the procedures should be.

What does due process require before long suspension or expulsion?

The courts have established no strict formula or procedure for all serious disciplinary matters. They generally hold, however, that prior to long term suspension or expulsion there must be a notice and a hearing; the accused student must be given the right to counsel and to cross-examine witnesses; and must also be given a statement of the findings, conclusion and recommendation, as well as the right to appeal.

The following is a model that has been suggested for use in serious cases[2]:

1. Notice of hearing, including
   a. the time and place
   b. a statement of the alleged infraction(s)
   c. a declaration of the student's right to legal counsel
   d. a description of the procedures to be followed in the hearing
2. Conduct a hearing, including
   a. advisement of student's right to remain silent
   b. the presentation of evidence and witnesses against the student
   c. cross-examination of the witnesses
   d. the presentation of witnesses on behalf of the student
   e. the recording (either by tape or in writing) of the proceedings
3. Finding(s) of hearing, including
   a. recommendation(s) for disciplinary action, if any
   b. report of findings to appropriate school authorities (e.g., the Board of Education) and to the student
4. Prompt application of disciplinary measure(s), if any, including the right to appeal.[2]

Do parents have the right to use lawyers in school disciplinary procedures?

That depends on the situation. As a general rule, in minor disciplinary matters, where the punishment is likely to be suspension for a short period of time, there is no right to be represented by a lawyer. On the other hand, if the likely punishment is long term suspension or even expulsion, students and parents can insist on representation by counsel. As in almost every other conflict, courts attempt to balance the competing interests of the schools against those of the parents and students. Because elaborate legal procedures for minor violations would be expensive, time consuming and cumbersome, relatively simple procedures are acceptable. On the other hand, when a severe punishment might befall a student, the balance tilts the other way, and fairness requires more careful, meticulous procedures.

May schools use corporal punishment?

Many parents are adamant that schools must never spank their children, while others subscribe to the time honored maxim, "spare the rod and spoil the child." Depending on where you live, the law may allow or forbid school officials to use corporal punishment.

The basic legal principle, established in common law and still with us today, is that a teacher or administrator may use such force as he reasonably believes to be necessary for the proper control, training, or education of the child. If the force is excessive or unreasonable, the educator in almost all states is subject to a civil suit for damages as well as possible criminal liability. In order to determine whether a punishment is reasonable, all the circumstances of the case must be considered. The important factors are: the seriousness of the offense; the student's attitude; past behavior, age and strength; the nature and severity of the punishment; and the availability of alternative, less severe means of punishment.

Of the 23 states that have legislation on the subject, 21 authorize the use of moderate corporal punishment in public schools. Some require that the parents be notified, some require an adult witness, and some permit only the school principal to administer the punishment. Only two states, New Jersey and Massachusetts, prohibit all corporal punishment in their public schools, but several cities, such as New York, prohibit it through local Board rules.

Where state laws or local rules do not prohibit it, courts have uniformly preserved the common law rule that permits the reasonable use of force to discipline children in schools.

May parents request that their children not be spanked?

Such requests can be made, but schools are not necessarily bound by them. Some states, like California, have laws that provide for prior parental approval in writing before corporal punishment can be administered. But where there is no such state law, schools do not have to get approval from parents. This was established by the Supreme Court in 1975, in the case of *Baker* v. *Owens*.[3]

Mrs. Virginia Baker of North Carolina had requested that her son's teachers or principal not use corporal punishment, because she opposed it in principle. Nevertheless, after her sixth-grader, Russel Carl, violated an announced school rule against throwing kickballs during certain times, he "received two licks in the presence of a second teacher and in view of other students."

Although the law of North Carolina allows the use of reasonable force "to restrain or correct pupils and to maintain order," Mrs. Baker claimed the law was unconstitutional since it allows such punishment over parental objections. The district court ruled against her, and when she appealed, the Supreme Court affirmed this ruling. While recognizing the basic rights of parents to supervise the upbringing of their children, the court also recognized "the state's legitimate and substantial interest in maintaining order and discipline in the public schools." Since both popular and professional opinion are divided on the question of corporal punishment, the court refused to allow "the wishes of a parent to restrict school officials' discretion in deciding the methods to be used in . . . maintaining discipline."

Is excessive punishment unconstitutional?

It is illegal but not unconstitutional, ruled the Supreme Court in 1977, in connection with a Dade County, Florida, case in which two junior high school boys were paddled until one of them "suffered a hematoma requiring medical attention and keeping him out of school for 11 days" and the other lost the use of his arm for a week. The parents of both boys claimed that this was cruel and unusual punishment and a violation of due process, since the boys had been given no prior notice and hearing.

By a 5-to-4 vote, the Court ruled that the 8th Amendment prohibition against cruel and unusual punishment does not apply to students, even when school punishment is excessive. After examining the history of cruel and unusual punishment, the Court explained that it was meant to apply only to criminal matters. Although the Court deplored excessive use of force in the schools, it concluded that adequate remedies are available against educators who use it, since they can be sued for money damages and even prosecuted in criminal action.

The Court further held that situations calling for corporal punishment do not require prior notice and hearing, or any other elements of due process, pointing out that the traditional common law remedy of suit for money damages is fully adequate against those who abuse their discretion as educators.

Parents who are dissatisfied with this ruling can reduce its effect on their children by working for state legislation or local board rules that will control educators in disciplining students. Parents who support the position of the Court, of course, have the same opportunities to influence state law and board rules.

May students and their lockers be searched?

As a byproduct of recent widespread drug use and violence in the schools, the practice of searching students' lockers and even their persons has become a highly visible issue. Public authorities not affiliated with the schools need a court order or a person's consent to search his house, person or car. Are school officials similarly bound in conducting searches in school?

In general, the answer is no. Courts have given broad leeway to teachers and administrators and have repeatedly held that the Fourth Amendment's protection against unauthorized searches does not apply to school lockers or even to the students themselves. In a New York case, for example, a judge said: "Not only have the school authorities the right to inspect but *this right becomes a duty when suspicion arises* that something of an illegal nature may be secreted there." [5] Courts in other states have come to similar conclusions.

But school officials do not have blanket power to search students' lockers at any time and for any reason. Such power, the courts have ruled, would be too broad and arbitrary. There must be a *reasonable suspicion* that drugs, weapons or other illegal or dangerous substances are hidden in the student's locker or on her person before a search can be conducted. A reasonable suspicion cannot be a mere hunch or a "fishing expedition." It must be based on observed facts or reliable information. Under these circumstances, school authorities may conduct the search themselves, or in collaboration with local law enforcement agencies. An increasing number of schools have established written policies on school searches and parents can request copies of these policies.

Some Other Aspects of School Discipline

May schools punish students for behavior away from school?

As a general rule they may not. But there are exceptions, such as school-sponsored field trips or athletic activities. Furthermore, if there is a close connection between schooling and the particular away-from-school misbehavior—as, for example, when a group of students attacked a girl a block away from school, on her way home—courts have upheld the rights of schools to administer reasonable discipline.

May your son or daughter be disciplined for breaking rules he or she didn't know about?

That depends. If the rules were generally known or if they were posted or available in student handbooks, your child can be held responsible for knowing them. The rules should be clear and understandable to ordinary students; rules that are too vague or overly broad will not hold up either in practice or in court, since students can't tell what is expected of them. For example, a rule calling on students "to behave and be good citizens" is so vague as to be useless and unenforceable.

May grades be lowered for improper conduct?

Increasingly, the courts are separating conduct from academic achievement. Since schools have procedures for dealing with improper conduct, grades, which are supposed to reflect school achievement, should not be altered by good or bad behavior. Many schools assign separate grades for conduct and for scholastic achievement.

In one case, a school attempted to withhold a student's diploma for alleged misbehavior. The court denied the school this right, pointing out that since the diploma is earned through academic achievement, poor behavior cannot be used to deny it. Separate disciplinary procedures are legitimate to address the question of misbehavior, but the diploma cannot be denied.[6]

Summary

During recent years, due process has become one of the most important constitutional rights of parents and students. In this chapter we focused on those aspects of due process that relate to disciplinary matters in schools.

As exclusion from schools, whether by suspension, expulsion or some other action, became a widely used form of discipline, parents and students challenged some school procedures, leading to a ruling by the United States Supreme Court that a minimum of due process is required even in cases involving short term suspensions. This, the Court said, is not an unreasonable burden for schools, since only such rudimentary elements of fairness as informal notice and hearing are required and this requirement is met if the student is told orally or in writing what his alleged wrongdoing was and what the evidence is against him, and if he is given a chance to tell his side of the story. In emergency situations, where there is danger to persons or property, the hearing will not be insisted upon until after the removal of the danger.

If a long term suspension or expulsion is the punishment, the courts require more complete procedures. In such situations you may insist on a notice and a hearing, and you have the right to be represented by a lawyer, to cross-examine witnesses and to be given a record of the proceedings. You also have the right to appeal—usually to higher school authorities and to the School Board. (A guidance conference is not a disciplinary action, nor is an ordinary transfer of a student from one class to another. But if a transfer is for purposes of punishment, due process should be followed.)

Constitutional attacks on corporal punishment have failed and it may be used by school officials, unless it is specifically forbidden by state or local law. However, no court protects unreasonable or excessive use of force. Educators who use excessive force can be sued for money damages, and can be subject to criminal liability. The Supreme Court has ruled that procedural due process is not required prior to corporal punishment. Parents should get to know the laws of their state and the local rules regulating corporal punishment, since they are usually more specific and helpful than court rulings based on the Constitution.

School officials may search student lockers or even the students themselves if they have a reasonable suspicion that illegal or dangerous drugs, weapons or other material is hidden there. They may cooperate with law enforcement officials, but must have a factual basis for their suspicions before they may proceed.

In general, your children cannot be punished by the schools for behavior away from school unless a clear and close connection can be shown to school activities. Students are held responsible for rules they should have known, even if they do not know them. And schools ought not lower grades or withhold diplomas for reasons of poor behavior.

History shows that parents and students have made significant gains in recent years in the recognition of their rights to due process. Many educators recognized these rights in the past, and today the courts, state laws and local policies are making them increasingly a part of the daily life of the schools.

Chapter 3
Freedom of Expression

During the first half of this century, the Bill of Rights rarely assisted parents and students who challenged the constitutionality of school rules. Courts generally used the so-called reasonableness test to judge school policies. If there was any reasonable relationship between the rule and the goals of the school, the rule would be upheld—even if many parents and educators believed it was unwise or unnecessary. Judges felt that school boards should have wide discretion and that courts should not substitute their judgment for that of school officials, who were presumed to be experts in educational matters.

In 1969, the U.S. Supreme Court handed down a historic decision that challenged the reasonableness test. In *Tinker* v. *Des Moines,* a suit initiated by a few concerned parents, the Court ruled that students do not shed their constitutional right to freedom of expression "at the schoolhouse gate." This chapter begins with a description of that important case, which changed the direction of education law in America. It then considers the extent and limits of a student's freedom of expression—in the classroom and on the playground, in school newspapers and underground publications.

The Tinker Case: A Landmark Decision [1]

In 1965, when the debate over American involvement in the Vietnam war was becoming heated, a group of students in Des Moines, Iowa, decided to publicize their anti-war views by wearing black armbands. Upon learning of the plan, the principals of the Des Moines schools established a policy prohibiting the armbands in order to prevent any possible disturbance. Although they knew about the policy, several students nevertheless wore the armbands to school and refused to remove them. They were then suspended. The parents of these students argued that the school policy was unconstitutional, and took their case to court. The judge ruled that the anti-armband policy was reasonable, but the parents did not give up. They pursued the case to the Supreme Court, presenting it with a conflict between the rights of students and the rules of the school.

While the Court recognized that school officials must have authority to control student conduct, it held that neither students nor teachers "shed their constitutional rights to freedom of speech or expression at the schoolhouse gate." The First Amendment protects symbolic as well as pure speech,* the Court said, and the wearing of an armband to express certain views is the type of symbolic act protected by that amendment.

Moreover, after reviewing the facts of the case, the Court found that there was "no evidence whatsoever" that wearing armbands interfered "with the school's work or with the rights of other students to be secure or to be left alone." School officials might have honestly feared that the armbands would lead to a disturbance, but the Court said that this fear was not sufficient to violate student rights. "In our system," wrote the Court, "undifferentiated fear or apprehension of disturbance is not enough to overcome the right to freedom of expression."

While the Court recognized that free speech in the schools may cause problems, it noted:

> "Any word spoken in class, in the lunchroom, or on the campus that deviates from the views of another person may start an argument or cause a disturbance. But our Constitution says we must take this risk; and our history says that it is this sort of hazardous freedom—this kind of openness—that is the basis of our national strength and of the independence and vigor of Americans who grow up and live in this relatively permissive, often disputatious society."

In a provocative comment about education and freedom, the Court wrote:

> "In our system, state operated schools may not be enclaves of totalitarianism . . . . Students in schools as well as out of school are possessed of fundamental rights which the State must respect, just as they themselves must respect their obligations to the State. In our system, students may not be regarded as closed-circuit recipients of only that which the State chooses to communicate."

In sum, the *Tinker* case held that school officials cannot prohibit a particular opinion merely "to avoid the discomfort and unpleasantness that

---

* See Appendix A for the wording of the First Amendment and other constitutional amendments most relevant to parents and students.

always accompany an unpopular viewpoint." On the contrary, unless there is evidence that the forbidden expression would "materially and substantially" interfere with the work of the school, such a prohibition is unconstitutional.* Thus the willingness of a few Iowa parents to assert the rights of their children led to a Supreme Court decision which expanded the rights of all students in the United States.

Does the Tinker decision apply only to the classroom?

No. The Court ruled that the principles of this case are not confined to the curriculum or to classroom hours. On the contrary, a student's right to freedom of expression applies equally "in the cafeteria, or on the playing field" and in all other school activities.

Can schools legally limit freedom of expression or symbolic speech?

Yes. There are limits to all constitutional rights. In *Tinker,* the Court stated that any student conduct which "materially disrupts classwork or involves substantial disorder or invasion of the rights of others is, of course, not immunized by the Constitutional guarantee of freedom of speech." Thus a federal appeals court upheld the rule of a Cleveland high school forbidding all buttons and badges because the wearing of some symbols had led to fighting between black and white students. Evidence indicated that if all symbols were permitted, racial tensions would be intensified and the educational process would be "significantly and substantially disrupted." [2]

Can your child be prohibited from discussing controversial issues in a student newspaper?

No, not just because they're controversial. In a Texas case involving an underground paper which discussed controversial subjects (such as current drug laws and where to get information about birth control, venereal disease, and drug counselling), a federal court ruled that "in a democracy 'controversy' is, as a matter of constitutional law, never sufficient in and of itself to stifle the views of any citizen." [3] Nevertheless, student publications may be limited in the "manner, place, or time" of distribution by reasonable and equally applied regulations. (E.g., schools may prohibit

---

* For a more complete report of the *Tinker* decision, see Appendix C.

distribution in classrooms, during assemblies or on crowded stairways.) But students cannot be punished for writing articles or distributing publications solely because they are considered controversial or because teachers, administrators, or parents disagree with their content. As one federal judge wrote: "... the purpose of education is to spread, not to stifle, ideas and views. Ideas must be freed from despotic dispensation by all men, be they robed as academicians, or judges or citizen members of a school board." [4]

Can students be required to submit publications to school officials for review prior to distribution?

Some courts have ruled that such requirements are an unconstitutional prior restraint. These courts acknowledge that schools can punish students who distribute materials that are libelous, obscene or cause substantial disruption; but they hold that administrators cannot require their approval in advance or prevent distribution.[5]

Other courts, however, hold that school rules can require prior review of student publications if the rules are clear and provide due process safeguards.[6] Due process requires that any rules for administrative review of publications before distribution must include: (*1*) a brief period of time for the review to take place; (*2*) clearly stated standards—e.g., definitions of obscenity, libel and disruption; (*3*) a reasonable method for appeal; and (*4*) the time within which the appeal must be decided.

Is the distribution of obscene or libelous materials protected by the Constitution?

No. But a publication is not obscene merely because it contains blunt, vulgar, or "dirty" words, nor is it libel merely because it is highly critical. According to current Supreme Court standards, material for students would be obscene only if the work (*1*) "appeals to the prurient interest" of minors, (*2*) describes sexual conduct "in a patently offensive way," and (*3*) "lacks serious literary, artistic, political or scientific value." [7] In applying these tests, the publication must be judged as a whole, rather than by particular passages selected out of context. Furthermore, school officials may not be able to object to certain vulgar language in student publications if the same language is found in books and articles in the school library.

A written statement about another person is libelous if it injures the person's reputation and if the writer knew or should have known that it is not true. A person who is libeled can sue for damages but truth is generally a defense against such a suit.

In short, student publications can't be banned simply because a school official thinks they are libelous or obscene; they can't, for example, be banned merely because they criticize the quality of teaching or use "dirty" words. But material that is, in fact, legally obscene or libelous is not protected by the First Amendment.

Can school officials control the content of publications if they pay the costs?

It depends on what is meant by "control." Administrators cannot censor student news and views, but they can decide whether or not to sponsor a student publication, and what level of financial support to give it. The limits of administrative control are not precise; but it is not total. Thus one court ruled that students could not be prohibited from placing an advertisement that was critical of U.S. government policy in a school-sponsored newspaper,[8] and another held that a student editor could not be prohibited from publishing responsible criticism about public officials.[9] In sum, school officials have some control over publications they sponsor, but they cannot suppress or censor student views or withdraw support from student newspapers simply because they do not like the views expressed in them.

Can schools prohibit students from inviting or listening to controversial speakers?

School officials apparently have authority to bar all outside speakers from school. But if they provide a forum for controversial outside speakers, they must allow opposing views to be presented and may not discriminate among proposed speakers or censor their ideas. In a high school where Republican and Democratic candidates were allowed to present their views, it was ruled unconstitutional for the principal to prohibit a Socialist Workers candidate from speaking.[10]

Summary

Since the landmark case of *Tinker* v. *Des Moines*, all courts recognize that the Bill of Rights applies to students in the public schools. Individual rights, however, are not absolute. When your child's right comes in conflict with the rights of other students or with the obligation of the school to keep order, judges weigh these competing interests in light of the circumstances of each case.

In *Tinker*, the Supreme Court held that restricting a student's freedom of expression is unconstitutional unless there is evidence that the forbidden conduct would "materially and substantially interfere" with school activities. Some courts have used the *Tinker* case to restrict symbolic expression where such symbols caused material disruption in the past or would probably cause an already tense situation to explode. On the other hand, courts have indicated that an "expectation of disruption" is not enough to justify suspension of your child's rights unless (*1*) such an expectation is "based on fact, not intuition"; and (*2*) school officials first make an honest effort to restrain those who might cause the disruption.

Before *Tinker*, administrators generally had "broad discretion" to censor school newspapers and punish students for distributing publications that "damaged school discipline" unless students could show that the school's actions were clearly unreasonable. This is no longer the law. Today, expression by public school students cannot be prohibited unless it substantially interferes with school activities or the rights of others. And if you question the constitutionality of rules that restrict your child's freedom of expression, it is up to school officials to justify the restriction.

This does not mean that the Constitutional rights of students are always the same as those of adults. Because there must be order as well as freedom of expression in the schools, authorities can impose reasonable restraints on the time, place and manner in which student publications are distributed. Nor does the First Amendment protect students who are abusive and seriously disrespectful to school officials or those who distribute materials that are legally obscene or libelous. However, the opinions of your children cannot be restricted nor can your children be punished solely because teachers, administrators, students, or other parents disagree with what they say or because the subject itself is unpopular or controversial.

Chapter 4
Freedom of Religion and Conscience

It is a generally accepted principle in our culture that parents have the right to determine and guide the religious upbringing of their children. This principle was given the force of law in 1925 when the Supreme Court upheld the right of parents to educate their children in parochial rather than public schools. After declaring that the State may not "standardize its children by forcing them to accept instruction from public teachers only,"[1] the Court stated: "The child is not the mere creature of the State" and thus placed in the hands of parents the right and even the obligation to guide the moral, religious and civic upbringing of their children. In this chapter we consider various issues involving religion and the public schools—among them court decisions related to religious objections to school attendance; controversies related to saluting the flag and reciting the Pledge of Allegiance; and others connected with prayers, Bible reading and silent meditation.

The Supreme Court's 1925 decision made it clear that parents could, if they chose, send their children to private schools, either religious or secular. But the question still remained: just how long must children attend school? If a given state requires children to attend school until the age of 16, may parents object to that requirement on religious grounds? This was precisely the question raised by several Amish parents who challenged Wisconsin's compulsory attendance law.[2]

Messrs. Yoder, Miller and Yutzy, devout members of the Amish community in Green County, Wisconsin, decided not to send their 14 and 15 year old children to school beyond the 8th grade. They believed that their own as well as their children's religious salvation would be jeopardized if the children attended high school and were exposed to a worldly and scientific curriculum that emphasized values quite different from those of the Amish community.

On the basis of their 300-year history of close-knit religious and communal life, the Amish believed that after their children mastered basic literacy in the elementary school, their further education should be occupational, and should take place on Amish farms and in Amish shops, under the close supervision of adult members of the community.

The State of Wisconsin, on the other hand, wanted to enforce its compulsory attendance laws, which required that students remain in school until they were sixteen.

The Supreme Court ruled in favor of the Amish parents, basing its reasoning primarily on the protection the First Amendment gives to the free exercise of religion, and citing its earlier decision protecting the right of parents to guide the religious development of their children. But this First Amendment right had to be balanced against the state's interest in having educated citizens. Here the evidence showed that the Amish youngsters had mastered basic school skills as well as the other students, had been given excellent vocational training in their own communities, and had an impressive record of general citizenship and self-reliance.

Since freedom of religion is one of the fundamental freedoms the Constitution guarantees, and since the evidence concerning the accomplishments of the Amish was quite favorable, the Court felt that the state's interest should not prevail. But the Court clearly warned that this type of exemption from the requirement of compulsory education would be only rarely granted. "It cannot be over-emphasized that we are not dealing with a way of life and mode of education by a group claiming to have recently discovered some 'progressive' or more enlightened process for rearing children for modern life." The exception granted the Amish was based on a demonstration that their religious beliefs and mode of life were inextricably related, that they had relied on these religious beliefs for three centuries, that they formed a successful and self-sufficient group in American society and that the enforcement of the state law would threaten their survival.

May parents object to flag saluting required by schools?

Yes, said the Supreme Court. In a west Virginia case,[3] Jehovah's Witness parents sued on behalf of their children, objecting to the daily flag salute required by state law. The Court, while recognizing the legitimate interest of the state in developing patriotic citizens and thus building national unity, ruled in favor of religious freedom, which it recognized as fundamental, to be overriden only by a compelling need of the state. In a powerful paragraph, Justice Jackson set forth a guiding principle of our nation:

"If there is any fixed star in our constitutional constellation it is that no official, nigh or petty, can prescribe what shall be orthodox in politics, nationalism, religion, or other matters of opinion or force citizens to confess by word or act their faith therein. If there are any circumstances which permit an exception, they do not now occur to us." *

Must all students recite the Pledge of Allegiance?

Courts have held such requirements to be unconstitutional.[4] If your son or daughter objects to reciting the Pledge of Allegiance out of religious conviction *or* as a matter of conscience, he or she does not have to participate in these exercises. Furthermore, schools may not require objecting students to stand during such ceremonies, or to leave the room, since this would be a mild form of punishment, and punishment should not be imposed for the exercise of a constitutional right. Of course, the non-participating student should be quiet and respectful and must not disrupt the patriotic exercise of the rest of the class.

May schools conduct daily prayers or read selections from the Bible?

No, they may not. The Supreme Court has ruled that Bible reading and school prayers violate the First Amendment's separation of church and state, and this ruling applies even if the prayers are non-denominational and participation is voluntary.[5] Furthermore, excusing students from participating in these exercises does not cure the constitutional defect because the prayers are still conducted under the auspices of the school and the school is an agency of the state. This ruling, made in 1963, still remains controversial and scores of schools and School Boards have violated it, by continuing prayers and Bible readings in the schools.**

---

* While the Court in this case upheld the right to refuse to salute the flag on the grounds of *freedom of religion*, more recent cases have indicated that the courts will rule similarly if someone objects as a *matter of conscience*, and in August 1977, a Federal district court declared unconstitutional a New Jersey law requiring all students to stand at attention during the recitation of the pledge of allegiance. The court ruled that such a requirement compelled "symbolic speech" in violation of First Amendment rights.

** It has been suggested that these practices constitute a form of civil disobedience and, by example, teach students that it is proper to violate the law on behalf of some higher moral principle. Is it inconsistent for educators and parents to violate the law against prayers in public schools and then object to other forms of civil disobedience, such as nuclear sit-ins, anti-war sit-ins, occupation of buildings, obstruction of court-ordered integration and others?

Is silent meditation or prayer allowed?

Some schools have made provisions for a brief period of silent meditation or prayer at the beginning of each school day. While the Supreme Court has never ruled on such a practice, a federal court in Massachusetts recently upheld a state law which established a daily "period of silence not to exceed one minute in duration . . . for meditation or prayer."[6] The District court saw no violation in such a law since each student could choose whether to pray in silence, meditate, or quietly think of anything at all.*

Other Controversies Concerning Religion and Education

Parents and students have raised religious objections to various aspects of the school curriculum and school activities from time to time in the past and objections are likely to crop up in the future as well. One high school student objected to participating in ROTC on religious grounds and a federal court ruled in his favor.[7] Similarly, a California court ruled in favor of parents who, for religious reasons, wanted their child exempted from folk dancing, which was required as part of the school's physical education program.[8] Parents have also raised religious objections to courses or school materials related to sex education and to the teaching of biology, evolution and theories of creation. The reader should examine Chapters *9* and *10* for decisions related to these topics.

Can parents conduct church-school at home in place of sending their children to public schools?

That depends on the laws of the state they live in and on the kind of home school they propose. In one Florida case the home school was disallowed on the grounds that it was not a school in the generally accepted sense of the word, and the parents involved were not qualified tutors under Florida law.[9] Parents who are interested in creating their own schools should, therefore, check their state laws carefully to be sure that the projects comply

---

* The word "meditation" brings to mind recent controversies over Transcendental Meditation (T.M.) in public schools. Whether or not T.M. is a religion is yet to be decided by the courts. Our use of "meditation" and its use in the Massachusetts statute refers to the secular meaning: "serious reflection or contemplation on a subject which may be religious, irreligious or nonreligious."

with minimal requirements. (For further discussion of this topic, see Chapter *10*.)

May children receive religious instruction during school hours?

Yes they may, but not in the public schools, and not from public school teachers. The Supreme Court has ruled it constitutional for schools to let students leave the campus during the school day for religious instruction as long as no school facilities or personnel are used and as long as all costs are borne by the religious organization.[10] The practice that has developed out of this ruling is known as "released time" religious education. A variation is the so-called "dismissed time" program, where all students are dismissed early on certain days and those who wish, go to religious education programs.

Can parents who send their children to private parochial schools expect the school to receive public funds?

The answer is yes and no, depending on the nature of the aid sought. In 1947 the Supreme Court upheld a state law by which New Jersey used tax funds to pay the bus fares of all pupils attending school.[11] Similarly a New York statute was upheld that provided for lending textbooks free of charge to all students, including those at private, parochial schools.[12] Neither of these rulings was unanimous, but both of them still stand.

Many other ways have been attempted to provide government support for the parochial schools—so-called parochiaid—and these efforts have aroused much controversy among parents. Under the efforts to grant parochiaid, state statutes have attempted to pay teachers' salaries, the cost of pupil testing, auxiliary school services, school maintenance and repair, tuition grants, tuition reimbursement and to give tax credits and pay other school costs. The Supreme Court has ruled each of these unconstitutional, a violation of the Establishment Clause of the First Amendment.[13]

On June 24, 1977 the Supreme Court handed down a major decision related to parochiaid. In ruling on a case that originated in Ohio, the Court held that states may finance therapeutic, remedial and guidance counseling for parochial school children *provided* that such services are rendered at a "neutral" site—that is off the school premises (at converted mobile homes, for example). On the other hand, diagnostic services, such as speech and hearing tests, can be provided in the parochial schools. Furthermore, states may provide parochial schools with standardized tests and test-scoring services, if they provide them to public schools.

In this same decision, the Court disallowed the financing of field trips for parochial school students as well as the provision of wall charts, slide projectors and other instructional materials.[14]

It is not exactly clear why it is proper to provide texts and transportation for parochial school students but not some other types of parochial school aid. Earlier decisions had claimed that texts and transportation benefit students, not the religion that supports the school. This so-called child benefit theory turned out to be very controversial, since it is difficult to draw the line between those benefits the students should have and those they should not, and the judges who opposed it argued that it would break down the wall of separation between church and state, as it applies to public schools. Today, the question by which the Court guides itself in these cases is whether the proposed arrangement has the "purpose or effect" of helping a religion and/or whether it leads to excessive "entanglement" between government and religion. The application of these tests excluded most parochiaid for elementary and secondary schools, while allowing for the provision of texts, transportation, testing and diagnostic and therapeutic guidance services at "neutral" sites.*

---

* This discussion does not apply to college level education. Courts have allowed certain kinds of financial aid to church-related colleges that might not be allowed to elementary and secondary schools. Similarly, clubs sponsored by religious organizations are allowed on public college campuses, but would not be allowed in primary or secondary schools.

Summary

From the earliest days of the Republic, disagreements have abounded concerning the proper relationship between religion and public institutions. Some parents have attempted to use public schools and public funds to further religion, while others have sought to keep the schools neutral and separate from religious influences. These conflicting efforts have inevitably ended up in the courts, and the Supreme Court has ruled on many aspects of the controversy.

The Court has ruled that although a state may require children to attend school, parents may satisfy this requirement by sending their children to private or public schools, and if private, either to religious or secular ones. Further, in the case of the Amish, the Court permitted parents to withdraw their children from school after the 8th grade, since the facts showed that the Amish religion would be significantly threatened by "worldly" high-school education. But this decision is not likely to apply to other groups. In the case of that sect, the Court was very impressed by its self-sufficiency and by the close relationship that has existed for more than 300 years between the Amish religion and the Amish way of life. Recently formed religious groups are not likely to succeed in their attempts to be exempt from schooling.

Students need not salute the flag or recite the Pledge of Allegiance if their objections are based on religion or conscience. But such students should not interfere with others' rights to participate in these exercises.

Courses on religion are perfectly legal, but prayers or Bible reading in schools have been declared violations of the First Amendment. However, the Massachusetts courts upheld a state law which allows a brief period of silent prayer or meditation. And ceremonial invocations and benedictions at graduation are also acceptable. The right of a student to be excluded from required high school ROTC has been protected and so have the objections of Jehovah Witness parents to their children's participation in folk-dancing in physical education classes.

Public funds for elementary and secondary parochial schools have, with some exceptions, been declared violations of the First Amendment. The exceptions make it legal for states to provide bus transportation for parochial school students, to lend them text books, and to provide diagnostic services, standardized tests and scoring services. The state may pay for therapeutic, remedial and guidance counseling services, provided they are rendered away from the parochial school at some neutral site.

Other efforts to secure parochiaid have been declared unconstitutional. Nevertheless, these efforts continue, particularly in state legislatures. It is safe to predict that controversy over the application of those sections of the First Amendment that relate to religion will be with us for many more years, for it is difficult to determine what constitutes an "excessive entanglement" that would threaten the high wall of separation between Church and State.

Chapter 5
Personal Appearance

Should parents have the right to allow their children to choose their own dress and hair style? Or should public schools be able to limit that right? Should the Constitution protect student grooming and clothing just as it protects freedom of expression? Or is the conflict over personal appearance a less significant issue?

The judicial response to these questions has been extraordinary. Controversies over grooming—particularly hair length—have provoked widespread disagreement not only among state and federal courts but among judges on the same court. The U.S. courts of appeals have issued conflicting rulings about the constitutionality of hair regulations, and the Supreme Court has declined to perform its usual role of resolving such differences. Therefore, this chapter will discuss and explain the conflicting judicial approaches to the regulation of grooming in the public schools. In addition, it will discuss a related question: dress codes and their legal status. Should students be able to choose their own dress style? Do schools have the right to limit that choice?

Grooming as a Constitutional Right: The Carpenter Case [1]

Indiana's Wawasee High School dress code was devised "to insure the best possible overall appearance" of the student body and was carefully developed by a committee of students, teachers and administrators. It was adopted by a vote of the students and they and their parents were clearly notified of its provisions before the beginning of the 1970 school year. Nevertheless, when school opened Greg Carpenter, with his parents' consent, chose to violate the code's "long hair provision." For this Greg was punished as the code provided—by being separated from his classmates and deprived of classroom participation until he cut his hair. As a result,

Greg's father sued on his behalf to prohibit enforcement of the code's hair length provisions. *

The school board argued that because the code was adopted by a majority of the students, it was not an unreasonable interference with Greg Carpenter's constitutional rights. But the Seventh U.S. Circuit Court of Appeals disagreed, holding that "the right to wear one's hair at any length or in any desired manner is an ingredient of personal freedom protected by the United States Constitution." To limit that right, a school would have to bear a "substantial burden of justification."

Here the board presented no evidence that Greg's hair disturbed classroom decorum or distracted other students, or that the hair provision was related to safety or health. To justify its interference with Greg's constitutional rights, the court said, the school must show a reasonable relationship between the code and some educational purpose, such as avoiding substantial disruption. Since such a relationship was not shown, the court concluded that the democratic process by which the code was adopted did not justify the denial of Greg's constitutional right to wear his hair as he chose. The U.S. Constitution, said the court, cannot be amended by majority vote of any school or community.

Related Decisions

Other federal appeals courts have given other reasons for supporting the concept of grooming as a constitutional right:

- In holding unconstitutional a Marlboro, Massachusetts school policy forbidding "unusually long hair," the First Circuit Court of Appeals wrote that the case involved "a very fundamental dispute" over the extent to which the Constitution protects certain "uniquely personal aspects of one's life." The court held that grooming was protected by the due process clause of the Fourteenth Amendment which "establishes a sphere of personal liberty for every individual," subject to restriction only if the exercise of that liberty interferes with the rights of others. The court saw "no inherent reason why decency, decorum or good conduct" requires a boy to wear his hair short. Nor, it concluded, does "compelled conformity to conventional standards of appearance seem a justifiable part of the educational process" [2]

---

* The code also contained a consent provision which allowed non-compliance if at the beginning of each semester a parent personally appeared before the principal and gave written consent for the exception of his child. Greg's father decided not to seek an exception for his son but to challenge the constitutionality of the code.

■ In striking down a St. Charles, Missouri restriction on long hair, one of the judges on the Eighth Circuit Court wrote:

"The gamut of rationalizations for justifying this restriction fails in light of reasoned analysis. When school authorities complain variously that such hair styles are inspired by a communist conspiracy, that they make boys look like girls, that they promote confusion as to the use of restrooms, and that the destroy the students' moral fiber, then it is little wonder even moderate students complain of 'getting up-tight.' In final analysis I am satisfied a comprehensive school restriction on male student hair styles accomplishes little more than to project the prejudices and personal distastes of certain adults in authority on to the impressionable young students." [3]

■ In a North Carolina case, Joe Massie was suspended because he refused to conform to grooming guidelines and because his hair length "evoked considerable jest, disgust, and amusement." [4] In its decision, the Fourth Circuit noted that, although in some situations long hair could be a form of symbolic speech entitled to the protection of the First Amendment, the Amendment did not cover Massie's case. He wore long hair simply because of personal preference, and, according to the court, had the right to do so as "an aspect of the right to be secure in one's person" guaranteed by the due process clause.

Was evidence that Massie's grooming had a disruptive effect enough to justify restricting his rights? No, because the disruptions were minor and probably could have been prevented. The Court observed that the school administration had made no effort to teach students that "there is little merit in conformity for the sake of conformity" and that a student may exercise a right any way he chooses so long as he does not "run afoul of considerations of safety, cleanliness and decency." The Court concluded that faculty leadership in "promoting and enforcing an attitude of tolerance rather than one of suppression or derision would obviate the relatively minor disruptions which have occured."

Upholding School Regulations: The Zeller Case [5]

The cases above reflect the reasoning of those courts that view grooming as a Constitutional right. The following cases are examples of judicial opinions which uphold the school's right to regulate student grooming. When Brent Zeller was excluded from a high school soccer team in Pennsylvania for noncompliance with athletic code hair regulations, his parents sued the school for violating their son's constitutional rights. But in a 1975 decision, the Third Circuit ruled against Brent and his parents.

The court declined to overturn the school regulations because it did not believe that federal courts are the right place to interpret "the conflicting ideals of student liberty and school regulation in the context of students' hair." On the contrary, the court said, in matters such as this, "the wisdom and experience of school authorities must be deemed superior and preferable to the federal judiciary's." Because our system of public education necessarily relies on the discretion and judgment of school administrators, federal courts should not attempt to correct errors "in the exercise of that discretion unless specific constitutional rights are violated. In this case, the court concluded that Zeller's complaint about the school hair regulations did "not rise to the dignity of a protectable constitutional right."

Related Decisions

■ Because 15 year old Robert Olff violated his California school's "Good Grooming Policy" (established by a student-parent-teacher committee), he was not allowed to enroll. As a result, Olff's mother asked the Ninth Circuit Court to declare the policy unconstitutional because it violated her son's "right of privacy." The court refused. [6] "The conduct to be regulated here," wrote the court, "is not conduct found in the privacy of the home but in public educational institutions where individual liberties cannot be left completely uncontrolled to clash with similarly asserted liberties of several thousand others." The court emphasized that this was not a question of preference "for or against certain male hair styles," but a question of the right of school authorities to develop a dress code in accord with their responsibility to educate. "A court might disagree with their professional judgment," wrote the judge, "but it should not take over the operation of the schools."

■ In upholding school grooming regulations, the Tenth Circuit wrote that the Supreme Court's recognition that students have constitutional rights does not mean that the Constitution "contains an express command that the hair style of a male student in the public school lies within the protected area." [7] The court was convinced that the Constitution does not impose on the federal courts "the duty and responsibility of supervising the length of a student's hair," and concluded that the problem "if it exists, . . . should be handled through state procedures."

■ Evidence presented at trial indicated that Michael Jackson and Barry Barnes wore their hair longer than permitted by school rules to enhance the popularity of their combo band and were a "distracting influence" in several classes during which they frequently combed and rearranged their hair.[8] Based on this evidence, the Sixth Circuit ruled that the enforcement of the school grooming code did not violate the students' constitutional rights.

■ The Fifth Circuit rejected the notion that hair regulations interfere with fundamental constitutional rights.[9] Even if these regulations interfere with a student's liberty, the interference is a "temporary and relatively inconsequential one." Furthermore, the court was disturbed by "the burden which has been placed on the federal courts" by suits such as this which took four full days of testimony, when many more important cases were kept waiting. Because of this burden and because these cases do not raise issues of "fundamental" liberty, the court announced that in the future, school grooming regulations should be presumed valid in all district courts in the circuit.

Why doesn't the Supreme Court resolve this conflict?

When federal circuit courts differ in their interpretation of the Constitutitn, the Supreme Court usually reviews the question, renders a decision, and thus establishes a "uniform law of the land." But despite the sharp differences of opinion among federal courts concerning student grooming, the Supreme Court has on at least nine occasions declined to review the decisions on this issue. This is because most justices of the Court apparently do not believe the cases raise important constitutional questions of national significance.

In rejecting an urgent appeal to the Supreme Court in one of the grooming cases, Justice Black wrote: "The only thing about it that borders on the serious to me is the idea that anyone should think the Federal Constitution imposes on the United States courts the burden of supervising the length of hair that public school students should wear." [10] As long as the Supreme Court refuses to hear these cases, the law will continue to vary throughout the United States.

What is the law in my state?

This depends where you live. In the First Circuit (Me., N.H., Mass., R.I.), the Fourth Circuit (Md., Va., W.Va., N.C., S.C.), the Seventh Circuit (Ind., Ill., Wisc.), the Eighth Circuit (Ark., Mo., Io., Minn., N.D., S.D., Neb.) and probably the Second Circuit (Vt., N.Y., Conn.) * the federal appeals courts have decided that grooming is a constitutional right. This means that parents who live in these circuits can go to court to challenge school grooming codes which restrict their child's hair length or style. In these states, grooming restrictions will be examined by the courts and can be declared unconstitutional unless school officials present convincing evidence that they are fair, reasonable, and necessary to carry out a legitimate educational purpose.

The law is different in the Fifth Circuit (Tex., La., Miss., Ala., Ga., Fla.), the Sixth Circuit (Oh., Mich., Ky., Tenn.), the Ninth Circuit (Wash., Ore., Calif., Alas., H.I., Nev., Ida., Ariz.), the Tenth Circuit (Wyo., Ut., Kan., Okla., N.M.) and probably in the Third Circuit (Penna., N.J., Del.) and the District of Columbia. **

In these states, the circuit courts of appeals have decided that grooming is not a significant constitutional issue and that the federal courts should not judge the wisdom of codes regulating hair length or style. This does not necessarily mean that you have no legal remedy if your child is disciplined for violating school grooming regulations. It only means that the federal courts will probably not consider your case. But you can still challenge the restrictions in state courts. And even if state courts uphold school grooming regulations, this only means that they are permitted, not required in your school district.

Clothing

Are school dress codes ever illegal?

Yes. Although schools clearly have the right to regulate student clothing, not all dress codes are legal. In New Hampshire, for example, a federal court held that a rule against dungarees was unconstitutional since the

---

* In 1973 the Second Circuit ruled [11] that hair length regulations raised "a substantial Constitutional issue." Although the U.S. Supreme Court overruled that decision as it applied to a policeman [12] the ruling probably would stand if it were applied to students.

** Although a recent decision of the Third Circuit [13] held that civilian employees of the National Guard could challenge the Guard's hair length regulations, the Court clearly ruled in 1975 [14] that "the federal courts should not intrude" in the area of school regulation of student hair length and that it would no longer consider school grooming cases. The D.C. Court of Appeals has not ruled directly on the issue of school grooming regulations, but it indicated in a related case [15] that it agreed with the U.S. Supreme Court and "sees no federal question in this area."

prohibition was not reasonably related to the school's responsibility or curriculum.[16] But although the court indicated that the freedom to wear the clothes of one's choice is a protected liberty under the Fourteenth Amendment, it did not hold that students could wear anything they wanted to school. As the judge observed, a school "can, and must, for its own preservation exclude persons who are unsanitary, obscenely or scantily clad."

Similarly a New York court annulled a high school's prohibition against girls wearing slacks because the rule enforced "style or taste and not safety, order, or discipline." [17] The court ruled that a board's regulation of dress was valid only to the extent necessary "to protect the safety of the wearer . . . or to control disturbance or distraction which interferes with the education of other students." And in Arkansas a judge held unconstitutional that part of a school dress code which prohibited all long dresses, frayed trousers, and tie-dyed clothing and required that all boys wear socks. These rules, said the court, were arbitrary, unnecessary, or overly broad.[18] On the other hand, the judge indicated that the following dress code provisions would be held valid: prohibitions against girls wearing "excessively tight skirts or pants" or dresses more than six inches above the knee (to prevent immodest clothing), prohibitions on boys wearing shirt tails outside their pants in "shop" (for safety reasons), or any student from wearing clothing displaying obscene pictures "or profane slogans or emblems." *

Will courts rule the same way in clothing cases as in hair controversies?

Sometimes. Those courts that do not protect a student's choice of hair style will probably not protect his choice of clothing. But courts that *do* protect hair style may not protect student freedom in matters of dress. Some courts hold that the constitutional liberty that guards a student's right to wear his hair as he wishes also protects his right to wear the clothing of his choice. Other courts, however, distinguish hair from clothing and indicate that restrictions on hair style are more serious invasions of individual freedom than clothing regulations. According to one judge: "the cut of one's hair style is more fundamental to personal appearance than the type of

---

* The court noted that "the overriding public interest in requiring the educators of our children to allocate their time primarily to the educational process supports the argument for permitting the adoption of easily enforceable and easily understood detailed standards as an alternative to broad general rules such as "all students shall wear clean, sanitary, safe, and decent clothing."

clothes he wears. Garments can be changed at will whereas hair, once it is cut, has to remain constant for substantial periods of time." [19] Thus some courts that recognize choice of hair style as a constitutional right do not protect choice of clothing style, and others give schools much wider discretion to regulate clothing in the interests of health, safety, order or discipline.

Summary

In an appellate decision concerning grooming, one federal judge observed:

> "Personal appearance, which comprises forms of dress and cleanliness, as well as hair styles, is merely one aspect of social behavior which the British broadly describe as 'manners'.... In the process of requiring the young to conform to the manners of their elders, parents and teachers are necessarily partners. If they agree that a child should be compelled to observe a given form of tradition, no matter how irrational it may be, the child has no legitimate recourse but to obey... It is only when the parent supports a child's attempt to accelerate a change in customs that a meaningful (legal) conflict arises."[20] *

As the cases in this chapter have illustrated, parents and educators frequently disagree about dress and hairstyle. Many parents support their children's changing customs, while others have joined with students and teachers to resist these changes. As a consequence, legal conflicts in this area have multiplied.

Grooming

Eight out of the eleven U.S. Circuit Courts of Appeals have clearly ruled on the constitutional right of students to choose the length of their hair.** As the map at the end of this chapter indicates, four circuits hold that grooming is a constitutional right that should be protected by the federal courts and four circuits do not. The arguments used on each side are varied and vigorous and no final decision establishing a uniform law has been reached, since the Supreme Court has refused to rule on the issue.

Upholding Student Rights. These are some of the constitutional arguments used to support a student's right to wear his hair as he wishes: A stu-

---

* Although minors rarely take legal action without the approval and support of their parents or guardians, a Michigan appeals court ruled that a 16-year-old student could sue his school district against his parents' wishes. The student was suspended because of his hair length, and he was represented by a Legal Services Attorney, appointed by the court under Michigan Court Rules which allow minors over the age of 14 and their representatives to bring suit without parental approval.[21]

** For an indication of how three other circuits probably would rule on this issue see footnotes on page 35.

dent's hair style is part of the personal liberty assured to citizens by the due process clause of the Fourteenth Amendment; the "freedom to govern one's personal appearance" is retained by individual citizens under the Ninth Amendment and it is part of the freedom of expression protected by the First Amendment.

In addition judges have offered these educational and philosophic arguments: hair regulations bear no reasonable relation to a legitimate educational objective; they teach conformity for its own sake; and they are not necessary for health or safety. Their enforcement projects the prejudices of certain adults in authority and causes more disruption than does the presence of long-haired students. If such students cause others to be disruptive, school officials should teach the disrupters tolerance and not suppress diversity. It is dangerous to say the problem is best left to local authorities; such a rationale could support any prohibition of parent or student rights.

Upholding School Rules. Among the legal reasons courts give for upholding school grooming regulations are these: The regulations seek to accomplish "legitimate objectives" and have "a real and reasonable connection" with the maintenance of school discipline; the Constitution does not protect grooming, but even if it does, it is one of the "lesser liberties" and not a fundamental right; and the "long hair" problem is "too insubstantive" to warrant federal court consideration.

In addition, judges upholding school regulations note that their purpose is to eliminate distracting extremes in hair style, to avoid possible conflicts, and to eliminate potential health and safety hazards. Even if some codes restrict student freedom, their effect is temporary and "relatively inconsequential" and still leave students a wide range of choice in grooming. School officials should have discretion and authority to develop dress codes without having to justify their professional judgment in court. Finally, all school regulations restricting student liberty cannot be litigated, for the judicial process is administratively unable to deal with the infringement of every minor right.

Clothing

Courts are divided on whether students have a right to wear the clothing of their choice. Most courts, including all those that support the right of schools to regulate hair length, hold that they do not. Each of the arguments used to reject the right of students to wear long hair has been used to reject their right to wear unconventional clothing. Moreover, some courts that protect student hair length reject students' claims to wear the clothing of their choice, justifying the distinction on the grounds that restrictions on hair style are more serious invasions of individual freedom: clothing can be easily changed after school, but if haircuts are required, the effect is more lasting.

A few courts protect clothing as well as grooming. Judges, for example, have ruled that flat prohibitions against boys wearing dungarees or frayed trousers, or girls wearing slacks or long dresses, are illegal because they are not reasonably related to the school's responsibility or its curriculum. Even these courts, however, recognize the validity of school regulations prohibiting certain kinds of clothing because of health or safety, or to prevent disturbance or distraction.

Compared to the "great grooming controversy," there are relatively few reported cases concerning clothing. As one federal judge observed, this may indicate that students, parents and administrators don't look on clothes with the same emotion with which they regard hair length or more probably "that most school boards are no longer concerned with what a student wears to schools as long as it is clean and covers adequately those parts of the body that, by tradition, are usually kept from public view." [22]

Now, towards the end of the 1970's, some readers may find it difficult to understand why so many students, parents and school officials were so concerned with the issue of hair length during the past decade. But the questions raised by these controversies involve far more than grooming; they concern such fundamental legal and educational issues as: When can school officials restrict student freedom? Should nonconformity be prohibited or guarded in our schools? Should courts protect individual choices or just "fundamental" freedoms?

In the coming years, hair length may no longer be the symbol that triggers this larger debate. But the basic issues will be with us as long as parents and educators continue to struggle with the problems of freedom and conformity in the public schools.

The following two pages contain a map of the Federal Judical Circuits.

☐ **School Restrictions Upheld**

Third Circuit
Fifth Circuit
Sixth Circuit
Ninth Circuit
Tenth Circuit
Eleventh Circuit

The Eleven Feder

Grooming As Constitutional Right
First Circuit
Second Circuit
Fourth Circuit
Seventh Circuit
Eighth Circuit
ial Circuits
MAINE
VT.
N.H.
MASS.
Boston
CONN.
R.I.
NEW YORK
New York City
PA.
Philadelphia
N.J.
DEL.
MD.
D.C.
Washington
W. VA.
VIRGINIA
Richmond
NORTH CAROLINA
SOUTH CAROLINA
GEORGIA
FLORIDA
ALABAMA
MISSISSIPPI
TENNESSEE
KENTUCKY
OHIO
Cincinnati
INDIANA
ILLINOIS
Chicago
MICHIGAN
CONSIN
URI
SAS
SIANA
New Orleans
CANAL ZONE
PUERTO RICO
VIRGIN ISLANDS
1
2
3
4
6
7
11

Chapter 6
Racial Discrimination and Education

Nearly a quarter of a century ago the Supreme Court of the United States declared that racial discrimination in the public schools is unconstitutional and the racial segregation of students is unacceptable. In the well known *Brown* [1] case, Chief Justice Warren announced the principle that has since become a nationwide standard:

> "In the field of public education the doctrine of 'separate but equal' has no place. Separate educational facilities are inherently unequal." [2]

While this general principle has become the accepted rule of law, disagreements over ways to carry it out have already spawned hundreds of law suits and promise to continue to be controversial in the future. In this chapter, we consider several important issues related to this aspect of schooling.

In the *Brown* case, the Court recognized that our national history of racial discrimination and segregation, together with wide variations in local conditions, would make any single remedy unworkable. Therefore, it called for arguments on the question of proper relief: the kind of order to issue to help schools overcome widespread, massive racial segregation.

The case known as *Brown II* [3] provides the general principles by which this question has been answered. Recognizing the diversity of local conditions, the Supreme Court assigned primary responsibility for desegregation to local school authorities, supervised by local courts, to ensure "good faith implementation of governing constitutional principles." Schools were to proceed reasonably and in good faith toward "compliance at the earliest practicable date" and to make progress, according to the now famous phrase, "with all deliberate speed." Since the speed in many communities matched that of a snail, lawsuits multiplied to enforce speedier compliance.

During the years since the *Brown* decision, parents have raised various questions concerning desegregation:

1. Must all schools be racially balanced according to some quota or ratio?
2. Must all one-race schools, whether all-black, all-white or all-yellow be eliminated?
3. Does the Constitution require that children be bused to achieve desegregation?
4. Are there limits to the redrawing of school district or attendance zones?
5. Why can't parents choose freely where their children attend school?

Some of these questions were raised in the *Swann* case.

Swann v. Charlotte-Mecklenberg Board of Education [4]

In 1965, the Charlotte-Mecklenberg school system of North Carolina placed a desegregation plan in effect. Under this plan, 84,000 students were enrolled in 107 schools during the 1968-69 school year. Of these, about 24,000 were black and of these black students 14,000 attended 21 schools that were at least 99% black. One of the black students, James Swann, with the support of his parents and others, requested the local school board to plan a more effective desegregation, since both he and his parents believed that many black students were not getting an equal educational opportunity in their racially imbalanced schools.

A proposed new plan by a court-appointed expert included controversial recommendations concerning grouping of schools and busing for racial balance, and went beyond the rezoning suggested by the school board.

> "... and desegregates all the rest of the elementary schools by the techniques of grouping two or three outlying schools with one black inner city school; by transporting black students from grades one through four to the outlying white schools; and by transporting white students from the fifth and sixth grades from the outlying white schools to the inner city black school.
>
> "Under the ... plan, nine inner city Negro schools were grouped in this manner with 24 suburban white schools." [5]

The dispute over this plan was appealed to the U.S. Supreme Court.

Must each school be racially balanced?

No, said Justice Burger, who wrote the opinion in the *Swann* case. "The constitutional command to desegregate schools does not mean that every school in every community must always reflect the racial composition of the school system as a whole." The Constitution does not require particular ratios or degrees of racial mixing. However, in school systems with a history of discrimination it is proper for the courts to make use of mathematical ratios as starting points in proposing remedies, though not as fixed requirements.

Must one-race schools be eliminated?

Not necessarily. Large cities tend to contain racial or ethnic neighborhoods in which one-race schools are often found, and the mere existence of these schools does not automatically constitute illegal segregation. But they should be carefully examined, Justice Burger urged, to determine whether or not they are the results of deliberate school assignments that create segregation.

Courts presume that one-race schools are the result of discrimination and school officials, therefore, have the burden of proving that students' assignments to such schools were genuinely nondiscriminatory. This is particularly the case in communities which in the past had dual school systems, one black and one white. As they change to unitary systems, they must satisfy the courts that their racial composition is not the consequence of past or present discrimination.

Is busing necessary for desegregation?

The big yellow school buses have become the controversial symbols of parental disagreements about desegregation. They have been used and abused, burned and destroyed in Massachusetts and Michigan, in Colorado, North Carolina, California and a score of other states.

Courts have applied the same general principles to the question of busing, as they have to other aspects of desegregation. Since conditions in different localities vary widely, no rigid rules can be laid down to govern all situations. The courts closest to the situation are, therefore, in the best position to consider such factors as local byways, traffic patterns, travel time, the ages of the children involved, health hazards, and costs to the school district. Any busing plan should be tailored to the particular needs of the situation.

Justice Burger noted that busing has played a significant role in the history of American education. In *Swann,* he wrote:

> "Bus transportation has been an integral part of the public education for years, and was perhaps the single most important factor in the transition from the one-room schoolhouse to the consolidated school. Eighteen million of the Nation's public school children, approximately 39%, were transported to their schools by bus in 1969-1970 in all parts of the country." [6]

Where should the line be drawn on busing to achieve desegregation? The

Supreme Court indicated that objections are valid when "the time or distance of travel is so great as to either risk the health of the children or significantly impinge on the educational process. It hardly needs stating that the limits on time of travel will vary with many factors, but probably with none more than the age of the students."

Can courts order busing across district lines?

In a suit brought by Detroit parents, the district court found a history of unconstitutional racial segregation and sought acceptable remedies.

In 1973, student enrollment in the Detroit school district was 69.8% black and 30.2% white. It was, therefore, impossible to achieve substantial racial desegregation *within* the city limits. On the other hand, since the 1970 census showed a metropolitan area racial composition of 81% white and 19% black, it was possible to draw up a desegregation plan which covered both Detroit and its suburbs—by sending some suburban children to city schools and some city children to schools in the suburbs. The district court accepted such a plan, and the appeals court upheld its ruling. The Supreme Court, however, disagreed in a 5-to-4 decision.[7]

Since the unconstitutional practices occurred in the city of Detroit, the majority of the court held that the remedy must be confined to the city limits. The dissenting four justices saw the situation differently. Since education is a function of the state government in Michigan, they wrote, the state had the primary responsibility to correct violations of the Constitution in schooling. Furthermore, since a proper remedy could not be achieved within the city limits of Detroit, they did not see sufficient reasons to respect municipal boundaries if this frustrated efforts to achieve school desegregation. But the majority prevailed and metropolitan area cross-district busing was struck down.

Does that mean that the courts can never require cross-district busing? No. Under certain circumstances, such busing is necessary and legally acceptable. This would be the case where district lines were purposely created to avoid racially mixed schools or where new districts were created to avoid court ordered desegregation.

As Justice Burger said in the Detroit case:

> "Before the boundaries of separate and autonomous school districts may be set aside by consolidating the separate units for remedial purposes or by imposing a cross-district remedy, it must first be shown that there has been a constitutional

violation within one district that produces a significant segregative effect in another district.

"Thus an inter-district remedy might be in order where the racially discriminatory acts of one or more school districts caused racial segregation in an adjacent district, or where district lines have been deliberately drawn on the basis of race. In such circumstances an inter-district remedy would be appropriate to eliminate the inter-district segregation directly caused by the constitutional violation. Conversely, without an inter-district violation and inter-district effect, there is no constitutional wrong calling for an inter-district remedy.[8]

Thus, remedies in desegregation cases must always consider the history of the community and its racial or ethnic composition as well as such factors as local geography, traffic patterns, highways, costs, special health hazards and certainly the age of the children.*

Can parents choose the schools their children will attend?

To some extent. As explained in Chapter 1, parents have the right to choose whether their children attend private or public schools, secular or religious ones. Furthermore, within the public school system, school boards and school officials may provide parents with a wide range of choices. This is not a legal matter but an administrative-educational policy to be determined in each community. But public schools are state agencies and board members, administrators and teachers are public officials and the policies they establish must be consistent with constitutional principles.

Parental freedom, for example, cannot be used to re-segregate the schools. Such arrangements were struck down repeatedly when the so-called "freedom-of-choice" plans were used as a subterfuge to continue segregated schooling. As the Supreme Court said in the *Green* case:

"Freedom-of-choice is not a sacred talisman; it is only a means to a constitutionally required end—the abolition of the system of segregation and its effects. If the means prove effective, it is acceptable, but if it fails to undo segregation, other means must be used to achieve this end. The school officials have the continuing duty to take whatever action may be necessary to create a 'unitary, non-racial system.' "[9]

Have the courts gone too far in taking over the schools?

Concerned parents as well as educators, lawyers and judges have raised this question in recent years, during which judges have exercised supervision

---

* Title 6 of the 1964 Civil Rights Act empowers the Attorney General to file suit on behalf of parents if they are denied equal protection for reasons of race, religion, sex, or national origin. See Appendix.

over such details of schooling as pupil and teacher placement, teacher and administrator selection, curriculum content, building maintenance, grading practices, and disciplinary procedures. In some instances receiverships have been created with court appointed "experts" in charge of schools and special "Masters" advising the judges.* [10]

These extreme measures are exceptional and are imposed on the schools only in highly unusual circumstances. Although the federal courts have wide-ranging powers, as a general principle they wish to avoid entanglement in educational policy and administrative activities. They are willing to examine these activities to see that they comply with the Constitution, but they readily admit their lack of competence in educational matters and they have no interest in becoming substitute school boards. Nevertheless, if a community has had a history of racial discrimination and if it exhibits a continuing resistance to desegregation, judges have wide discretion in the means and methods at their disposal to enforce the law. It is never a happy solution when courts exercise substantial supervision over the details of schooling, but it may be legally necessary. Such situations are always highly controversial, with parents on each side of the controversy.

Must schools continually redraw attendance lines?

If after a community desegregates its schools, population changes again create racial imbalance, must the school board redraw attendance lines to compensate for such imbalance? In a Pasadena case, the Supreme Court said no.[11]

Justice Rehnquist, who wrote the decision, relied on the *Swann* case (see page 45), and stated that the duty to rearrange attendance zones exists only as long as there is a constitutional violation. Once the duty to desegregate has been satisfied, there is no further constitutional requirement to make year-by-year adjustments.

* The recent history of the Boston schools exemplifies some of these arrangements.

Summary

For over twenty years, since the landmark *Brown* case, it has been an established principle of our government that segregated education violates the 14th Amendment of the Constitution. The problems of implementing this principle have turned out to be many and very controversial.

In many localities, racially mixed schooling is difficult to achieve without massive transportation of students, and busing children to desegregate the schools has emerged as the most controversial issue in education in recent decades. However, as the Supreme Court ruled in the *Swann* case and has reaffirmed in subsequent cases, busing is a legitimate means to achieve desegregation in school districts with a history of racial segregation.

It is quite possible, however, that if white flight continues, increasing the percentage of racial minorities in the cities, desegregated schooling *within* city limits will be unworkable. This was the case in Detroit where a proposal was made that would achieve desegregation by busing across district lines. The Court struck down this proposal and said that the remedy must be applied only to the school district where the constitutional violations occurred. Cross-district busing for desegregation will be required only where the formation of separate districts has created or aggravated racially separate schooling.

It seems highly probable that the twin concerns of parents—neighborhood schooling and desegregation—will continue to bring cases to court into the indefinite future. On the other hand, many communities have achieved desegregated schooling through cooperative, non-legal means without recourse to the courts. Those disagreements that do reach the courts will probably be resolved by relying on the following Supreme Court principles from the *Swann* case: *(1)* To achieve "racial balance" mathematical ratios can be used as guides, but not as fixed quotas. *(2)* Attendance zones may be altered and schools may be "paired," "clustered" or "regrouped" to eliminate dual school systems. *(3)* One-race schools are not necessarily unconstitutional, although the presumption is against them and school officials have the burden of proving that assignment to them is non-discriminatory. *(4)* Busing is a legitimate means to desegregate schools, and its limits will be set so that the time and distance traveled will not be detrimental to the health and education of children.

Literally hundreds of decisions could be cited consistent with these principles. They have been handed down in all parts of the country, north and south, rural and urban. The ways desegregation is carried out must always be tailor-made to the unique features of the school district involved, but still must be consistent with the principles of the *Brown* case, decided over two decades ago.

Chapter 7
Sex Discrimination In The Schools

More than half the students in our public schools are female, and more than half of the teachers are women. Even so, various areas of school life have historically discriminated in favor of male students. Until quite recently schools commonly restricted certain courses to boys only, provided preferential treatment to boys' athletic activities, suspended or expelled pregnant students and treated boys and girls differently in other school-related activities.*

Have these policies and practices been changed or eliminated? Must your sons or daughters be treated identically by your public schools or can some school practices be legitimately influenced by considerations of sex? In this chapter we look at cases related to these and other issues involving sexual discrimination and stereotyping. We also discuss Title IX,[1] a federal law that has become a powerful means for eliminating sexual discrimination from the schools.

Athletic Activities

High school interscholastic sports are highly organized in the U.S., and in most states are regulated by state-wide league rules. Minnesota's high schools were regulated by the Minnesota State High School League, which had the following rules:

> "Girls shall be prohibited from participating in the boys' interscholastic athletic program either as a member of the boys' team or a member of the girls' team playing the boys' team. The girls' team shall not accept male members."

Despite this rule, Peggy Brenden wanted to play on her high school's boys' tennis team. She was an outstanding player, ranked number one

* Boys, too, have been discriminated against in school—forbidden, for example, by some authorities to take cooking or sewing courses. But by and large they have faced far fewer problems because of their sex than girls have.

among the 18-year-olds in her area during 1972. Since there was insufficient interest in tennis among the girls of her school, there was no girls' team and thus no interscholastic competition for Peggy. By contrast, the boys had a team, a coach, and a regular schedule of matches. School officials, citing the League rules, refused Peggy an opportunity to compete for a place on the boys' team.

Peggy and her parents went to court claiming that her civil rights and her rights to due process and equal protection had been violated. Her case was heard together with the case of Tony St. Pierre, a 17-year-old female student at the Eisenhower High School, in another Minnesota school district, who had been denied the right to compete on the boys' cross-country running and cross-country skiing teams.[2]

The school districts maintained that the League rule was reasonable and protected the fair and orderly conduct of interscholastic athletic competition. Furthermore, they claimed that such competition was a privilege, not a right, and therefore could be regulated by the schools.

In deciding this case, the court acknowledged the substantial differences between boys and girls, which in general favor boys in athletic competition. On the other hand, it also recognized that Peggy and Tony were exceptional cases. So, although the court did not declare the League rules inherently unconstitutional, it did strike them down in their application to these two young women. In the words of the court:

> "It must be emphasized in this case, however, that these physiological differences, insofar as they render the great majority of females unable to compete as effectively as males, have little relevance to Tony St. Pierre and Peggy Brenden. Because of their level of achievement in competitive sports, Tony and Peggy have overcome these physiological disabilities. There has been no evidence that either Peggy Brenden or Tony St. Pierre, or any other girls, would be in any way damaged for competition in boys' interscholastic athletics, nor is there any credible avidence that the boys would be damaged." [3]

A rule can be unconstitutional by *itself,* if, for example, it is arbitrary or unreasonable or if it denies equal protection. Or it can be unconstitutional *in its application.* The latter was the ruling in the Minnesota case. In other words, the court found that these two exceptional women athletes were prevented from participating in interscholastic activities "on the basis of the fact of sex and sex alone." Since the school provided no alternative competitive programs for them, the rules were declared unreasonable and discriminatory, as applied to Peggy and Tony, and the girls were declared eligible to compete on the boys' teams. Moreover, the state High School

League was forbidden to punish the schools on whose teams the girls would compete.

Must schools provide opportunities for interscholastic athletic competition for both male and female students?

Not necessarily. Public schools do not have to provide such activities at all. That is a policy to be decided by each state, or, in the absence of state laws, by each school district. But if a school district provides such opportunities, they must be available to all on equal terms. If, for example, a school has only a boys' team for such noncontact sports as golf, tennis or swimming, girls have the right to try out for positions on the teams.

What if there are teams for boys and girls? Can a superior girl athlete try out for the boys' team if the girls' team doesn't provide enough of a challenge for her? Not in most states. In the absence of specific state laws or regulations, courts have ruled that separate teams and leagues for boys and girls are reasonable and not discriminatory. Many educators support this separation as the best way to encourage both boys and girls to participate in athletics. Although it does not benefit the exceptional female athlete, it does help the average girl. Certain states—Michigan and New York, for example—have gone further than the courts, making girls eligible for membership on boys' non-contact sports teams even in schools where girls' teams exist. Another alternative would be the establishment of both a top team based solely on ability and separate teams for boys and girls to encourage broad participation. But budgetary considerations lead most school boards to establish only two teams: boys' and girls'.

Until now, we have been talking about non-contact sports. What about contact sports such as football, baseball or hockey? There have been fewer cases in this area, but in Pennsylvania, where the Equal Rights Amendment has been voted part of the state constitution, a court ruled that both boys and girls can try out, on an equal basis, for all athletic teams, including those in contact sports.*

Title IX: Equal Resources for Athletics?

Must schools provide identical amounts of money for the support of male and female sports?

---

* In the other 12 states which have added the ERA to their constitution, this issue has not yet been brought to court.

Generally, no. Historically, most of our schools and school districts have given much larger budgetary allotments to male athletic programs than to female ones and on the whole male students have tended to participate more in sports than females. So most people thought it senseless for schools to provide identical resources for male and female athletics.

It is probably true that these limited opportunities and expenditures were themselves part of the reason that girls participated less in sports. But there is some evidence that this situation is changing. There are, however, no authoritative court rulings on the question of equal expenditures for female and male athletics.

The federal legislation commonly known as Title IX may prove to be the most effective means to bring about equality in budget and other allocation for athletics. It provides that:

> "No person in the United States shall on the basis of sex be excluded from participation, be denied the benefits of, or be subjected to discrimination under any education program or activity receiving Federal financial assistance."

Moreover, its regulations specifically refer to athletic programs and forbid discrimination in the provision of supplies, equipment, facilities and supporting services of various types. While these regulations clearly require equal treatment, they also recognize that there is not always sufficient interest among students to form teams for males and females. In such situations, the law is satisfied if males and females each have fair opportunities to compete for positions on the same team.

In addition to Title IX, which is federal law, many states have passed legislation requiring more equitable treatment of female athletics in public schools. Parents should get to know the laws of their own states as well as the national law and the Constitution, since state laws are often more specific and helpful.[4] In fact, although we have focussed our discussion on athletics, the same principles apply to other school activities; we have paid less attention to questions of sex discrimination in the curriculum and the availability of courses and programs because such practices quickly crumble before the law. Some states, such as New York and Massachusetts, have passed laws prohibiting the exclusion of students from any course of instruction by reason of sex. In states which have no such laws, suits have been brought against these practices. In every case, the suits have been quickly settled and the practices have been changed.

This is not to say that all schools currently practice equal treatment of boys and girls. Tradition, ingrained customs and habits are difficult to change. Many parents, for example, believe that girls should stay out of shop courses and boys out of cooking and sewing. There are also those who think that girls should not compete for positions on the boys' tennis or golf teams. So, even when laws and official policies support equal opportunities, the informal pressures of a school and the community often discourage equal participation by male and female students.

May public schools provide separate schools for boys and girls?

Yes, answered a Pennsylvania court, if the schools are provided on an equal basis to both male and female students.[5] The wisdom or educational value of such separation is not a legal question, the court said, and courts do not take stands for or against such arrangements, since they are basically the concern of educators and parents and perhaps students. As long as they do not establish unfair or discriminatory treatment of either group, the courts are not likely to substitute their wisdom for that of the school and the parents.*

May different standards be used for the admission of boys and girls to school?

A Boston case said no. In 1970, Boston Latin School had two separate buildings. Boys Latin with a capacity of 3,000 students and Girls Latin with a capacity of 1,500. Each year, the city school department determined the necessary entry scores on the written examination for each by first checking the number of vacancies in each building. In 1970, girls had to score 133 to be admitted, while boys had to score 120. The court held this arrangement to be a violation of the Equal Protection Clause of the Fourteenth Amendment.[6] A similar decision was reached in a San Francisco case in 1974.[7] Title IX also prohibits such practices.

May schools expel pregnant students?

In the past, most people agreed that married or pregnant students should

---

* Various commentators have noted that the doctrine of "separate but equal," which was struck down when the separation is based on race, seems to be acceptable when it is based on sex, if there are legitimate educational reasons for the separation. As yet, the Supreme Court has not ruled on this issue directly. But where it has heard cases involving sex discrimination, it has not applied as rigorous standards as it has in cases of racial discrimination.

not continue attending school, on the grounds that pregnant girls or married students disrupted school activities, that sexual relations among teenagers was immoral and that pregnant girls and married students were physically and psychologically better off away from school.

In recent years this trend has been reversed. Although some school boards and educators would still exclude married or pregnant students from high schools, more and more believe that these students need education and that their "corruptive influence" has been grossly exaggerated. And courts have held that where a state provides public schools for teenagers, pregnant and married students have a right to attend.[8] Furthermore, Title IX regulations specify that if a school offers a separate program for pregnant students, it must be comparable to that offered for non-pregnant students.

In an effort to discourage early marriages, some schools still bar married students from extracurricular activities, athletics and student offices. In 1959, a Texas court upheld such a school rule. The court made no judgment on the wisdom of the rule, but merely said that it was a matter for the Board of Education and that it would not interfere unless the school rule was arbitrary and unreasonable.[9]

On the other hand, different results were reached in more recent cases in Texas,[10] Ohio,[11] and other states. Courts now find extracurricular activities to be an important part of the school program and ask whether the student's marriage interferes with school discipline in a material and substantial way. If it does not, the court considers the rule to be arbitrary and protects the student's right to participate in the activity.

Since Title IX specifically forbids discrimination either in class or in extracurricular activities because of a student's marital status or pregnancy, there should be very few such law suits in the future.

It must be pointed out, nevertheless, that many girls still drop out of school as a result of marriage or pregnancy. Many communities seem unconcerned when this happens, and make little effort to help the girls continue their education.

Must the school faculty and staff be sexually integrated?

Title IX regulations forbid discrimination in employment in schools, except military schools and those religious schools where compliance would violate religious tenets. Thus, schools that receive or benefit from federal funds must incorporate principles of Affirmative Action* and must not discriminate in recruitment, hiring, promotion, tenure, job assignment or any other aspect of employment. From the perspective of parents, it could be said that there is a right to a teaching faculty and staff that are sexually nonsegregated.

* Affirmative Action means that schools must make positive efforts to search for and find qualified female and minority personnel to fill job vacancies. This policy goes further than nondiscrimination, which requires only that schools do not discriminate among applicants. It places a responsibility on schools to increase their efforts and broaden their search for candidates who belong the groups that are underrepresented on their faculties or in leadership positions.

Summary

Court cases as well as federal and state laws have made significant gains in reducing sexually discriminatory practices in schools during recent years. While all aspects of schooling have felt the influence of such changes, perhaps the areas of greatest significance to parents fall under three headings: (*1*) female students' access to sports, (*2*) equality in admission and in the curriculum, and (*3*) schooling of married or pregnant students.

Sports

Even though schools still provide more athletic activities for male than for female students, progress has been made toward equality in sports. The discrepancy might well be the function of tradition and the slow rate at which some habits change.

Schools do not have to provide inter-scholastic athletics. But if they have such teams, as a general rule they must be made available to both girls and boys on a nondiscriminatory basis. This means that in non-contact sports schools could have separate teams for boys and girls, each with proper equipment, coaching and other support services. If only boys' teams are available, girls must have opportunities to compete for positions on them. Some states have gone further and by state law or constitutional amendment have provided opportunities for girls to try out for boys' teams even when there were separate teams for boys and girls. Some states have even opened up contact sport participation to males and females alike. Title IX also mandates nondiscrimination in supplying equipment and resources to the athletic programs of both sexes.

Admission, Curriculum, and Counseling

In recent years public schools have tended to be co-educational, and admission policies have not been based on sex. But occasional cases have arisen. One of these, a Pennsylvania case, upheld the right of a school district to provide for separate schools for boys and girls as long as such schools were equal in quality. In a Massachusetts case, admission practices to Boston Latin Schools were struck down, because girls had to score higher than boys on a standardized test to get in.

In the past, the curriculum contained many sexually segregated classes.

Girls often could not take woodwork or auto shop, and boys were often excluded from cooking, sewing and even typing. These practices are fast disappearing and they are clearly illegal. Books and other school materials are increasingly examined to eliminate sexual stereotyping and most counselors no longer offer vocational advice on the bases of sex alone. But when discriminatory practices continue by informal means, "friendly" advice and subtle pressures, parents can change them more effectively than courts or legislatures.

Pregnancy and Marriage

In the past, most girls who got married or pregnant dropped out of school. School policies encouraged and often required them to do so. Some schools still have policies discouraging teenage marriages and pregnancies, though increasingly these are being challenged.

States with compulsory attendance laws specify age limits for schooling. Within those age limits, students have a right to attend school even if they marry, and the same holds true if they become pregnant.

The law is in conflict regarding the rights of married and pregnant students to participate in extracurricular activities, or hold student offices. Some courts have upheld school rules that prevented married students from participating in athletics, while courts in other jurisdictions have held such rules to be arbitrary and unreasonable. It seems to us that courts are increasingly protecting the rights of married or pregnant students to full participation and completion of their schooling. But in some of these matters, the courts will respect the discretion of local school boards; therefore, it becomes very important for parent groups to make their opinions known and do what they can to influence local school policies.

Chapter 8
Student Injuries: The Right to Compensation

Schools have a clearly established legal duty to provide students with safe facilities and adequate supervision. If your son or daughter is injured because of the negligence of a teacher or other school employee, you may be entitled to compensation. But this does not mean that schools are responsible every time a student is hurt. How can parents know when a school employee is legally negligent? Does negligence always lead to liability and compensation? Can parents sue teachers or administrators for making false and damaging statements about their children or for violating their constitutional rights? These are some of the questions that were raised in the cases in this chapter, all of which fall into the general area that lawyers call the law of torts.

When Is a Teacher Negligent? The Sheehan Case [1]

Margaret Sheehan was an eighth-grade pupil at St. Peter's School. One spring morning during recess, a teacher took Margaret and nineteen other girls to an athletic field where a group of eighth-grade boys were playing baseball. After directing the girls to sit on a log on the third-base line, the teacher returned to the school building. About five minutes after she left, some of the boys began to throw pebbles at the girls. Although the girls protested, the boys continued until one of the pebbles struck Margaret in the right eye, seriously injuring her.

Margaret's parents sued for damages on her behalf, claiming that the school and the teacher were negligent in failing to supervise the children's recess adequately, since the teacher was absent from the athletic area from the time she brought the girls there until after the accident.

After both sides presented their case, the judge instructed the jury: "It is the duty of a school," he said, "to use ordinary care and to protect its students from injury resulting from the conduct of other students under circumstances where such conduct would reasonably have been foreseen and could have been prevented by the use of ordinary care." But, the judge said, "there is no requirement of constant supervision of all the movements of the pupils at all times."

The jury, whose duty it was to apply the law to the facts as they found them, found that it was reasonable to foresee that a student might be hurt as a result of failure to supervise the athletic area and decided that the school was negligent. The school appealed on the grounds that there was no proof that watching boys play baseball had been dangerous in the past or that supervision would have prevented the accident.

The appeals court ruled in Margaret's favor on the grounds that children have a "known proclivity to act impulsively without thought of the possibilities of danger," and that it is precisely this lack of mature judgment that makes supervision vital. " The mere presence of the hand of authority," wrote the court, "normally is effective to curb this youthful exuberance and to protect the children against their own folly."

Does this mean that a teacher is expected to anticipate every situation where one child may suddenly injure another? No. The law does not expect a teacher to prevent an unforeseen injury that could happen quickly and without warning. But this was not such a case. Here the girls protested when the pebble throwing began, and the boys continued pelting the girls for several minutes before Margaret was injured. Under these circumstances, the jury concluded that a teacher using reasonable care would have stopped the boys and prevented the injury and that the teacher was therefore negligent in leaving the athletic field unsupervised.

Is constant supervision required?

Two teachers in Chicago's Medgar Evers School organized a trip to the city's Field Museum of Natural History for about fifty students, ranging from 12 to 15 years of age.[2] When they arrived at the museum, the students were allowed to divide into smaller groups and look at the exhibits without supervision. While away from the teachers, Roberto Mancha was beaten by several boys who were not connected with the school.

Roberto's parents charged that the teachers who organized the trip were negligent in failing to supervise their students in the museum. Clearly the teachers were required to exercise reasonable care on such a trip. But the question posed by this case is whether that duty extended to foreseeing and guarding against the injury that occurred. This would depend on the the likelihood of injury, the size of the burden of guarding against it, and the consequence of placing that burden upon teachers.

In this case, the court considered the risk that a 12-year-old boy would be assaulted in the museum as minimal, and the burden that would be imposed on the teachers in guarding against it heavy, since it would require constant surveillance. Such a burden would discourage teachers from providing many useful and enjoyable extra-curricular activities, since a baseball game or even a game of hopscotch could suddenly break into a fight that produced serious injury.

This does not mean that teachers are never required to provide constant supervision on a field trip. On the contrary, the court indicated that such supervision would be required when students are taken to a stone quarry, a place where there is dangerous machinery, or where there is reason to believe an assault might take place. But the museum was a "great educational enterprise" for teachers and students, not a place of danger. Under these circumstances, the teachers did not have a duty to anticipate an assault or directly supervise the entire museum trip among 12-to-15 year-old students.

When must students be warned?

In addition to providing supervision, teachers have a duty to instruct and warn students concerning the proper use of equipment and facilities, whether in class, gym, shop, or anywhere else in the school. Failure to do so constitutes negligence. Thus, a physical education teacher was found negligent for allowing two boys to engage in a "slugging match" because he failed to give instructions in self-defense to any of the students.[3] Similarly, a chemistry teacher was found negligent when she failed to instruct students in the proper precautions to follow while carrying out an experiment in the production of explosive gases.[4] And a Wisconsin court found negligence in the case of a 21-year-old vocational student who was injured while operating a complicated high speed machine without being given proper instructions.[5]

How careful must schools be?

The legal principles applied in cases like these are clear: Teachers and other school employees have a duty to exercise reasonable care not to injure their students and to prevent them from being injured. Reasonable care is that degree of care that a reasonable teacher of ordinary prudence would exercise under the circumstances. The circumstances considered would include the age, maturity and experience of the students and the extent of danger involved. Whether a teacher exercised reasonable care is a factual issue, decided by the jury or the trial judge.

When circumstances are obviously dangerous, as in shop or physical education, a teacher would be expected to exercise greater care than in, for example, the mathematics class. A teacher's failure to be more careful when the dangers are greater—to provide closer supervision, clear warnings, and careful instructions—would constitute negligence.

In the case of Margaret Sheehan, it was decided that the teacher did not exercise reasonable care in leaving Margaret and her classmates at the baseball game without supervision. In the case of Roberto Mancha, however, the court did not feel that reasonable care required the teachers to provide constant supervision of all the students while they were examining the exhibits in the museum.

What is legal cause? The Nash case.[6]

Many parents believe that if a school employee is found negligent, she is automatically liable for damages. The case of Wilmer Nash shows that the parents of an injured student must show more than negligence to recover—they must also show that the employee's negligence was the cause of the injury.

After school one day, Wilmer, a Louisiana elementary school pupil, was waiting with a group of classmates for the school bus to take him home. While waiting, Wilmer was struck in the face with a stick carried by a little girl who was playing near him. The blow left Wilmer blind in his left eye, and his parents sued the school for failing to provide adequate supervision.

The court acknowledged that schools are required to provide supervision while pupils are waiting for the school bus. And the evidence indicated that the teachers had failed to provide any supervision at the time Wilmer was injured. But the court did not find either the school or the teachers liable. Wilmer's attorney was not able to prove that proper supervision would have prevented the injury—that, in other words, there was a causal connection between the absence of supervision and Wilmer's accident.

"How," asked the judge, "could any teacher anticipate a situation where one child, while teasing another child, would be struck in the eye with a stick by a third child?" Even if such action could have been anticipated, there was no evidence that the injury could have been prevented if a teacher had been present. "As is often the case," concluded the judge, "accidents such as this, involving school children at play, happen so quickly that unless there was direct supervision of every child (which we recognize as being impossible), the accident can be said to be almost impossible to prevent." Thus the court ruled in favor of the school because Wilmer's parents had failed to show any causal connection between the absence of supervision and the accident that occurred.

A Basketball Injury. A similar case arose in New York where a student was seriously injured when he jumped for a basketball and bumped heads with another student.[7] The parents of the injured student sued the school for failure to provide proper supervision. But the court ruled that there was no "legal causal connection" between the absence of supervision and the injury. The presence of a teacher would not have stopped the boys from bumping their heads together. "That," said the court, "is one of the natural and normal possible consequences or occurrences in a game of this sort which cannot be prevented no matter how adequate the supervision."

Thus, these cases indicate that in order to hold a school employee liable for your child's injury, you have to prove both that the employee was negligent *and* that there was a causal connection between the negligence and the injury.

Do schools have defenses against liability?

Yes. Parents suing for damages on behalf of their injured child may find the following defenses raised against the charge: contributory negligence; assumption of risk; or governmental immunity.

Contributory Negligence. A negligent teacher might not be held liable if a student contributed to his injury by his own negligence. For example, although a school bus driver was acknowledged to be negligent in failing to repair a hole in the floor of his bus, the court held that he was not liable for damages when it was shown that the student who was injured had deliberately stuck her foot through the hole for amusement, and was, therefore, contributorily negligent.[8] Similarly, a janitor who negligently unlocked a chemical supply room was held not liable for the injury suffered by a 17-year-old high school student who carelessly experimented with chemicals stolen from the unlocked room.[9] Thus, if a student fails to exercise that degree of care usually expected of a person of his age, knowledge and experience, his contributory negligence may prevent recovery from a negligent employee.

If a student is negligent, does this always prevent recovery?

No. The younger the student, the more difficult it is to improve contributory negligence. Generally, courts will presume that students under 14 are not negligent, but with sufficient evidence this presumption can be rebutted. On the other hand, many courts presume that very young children are by definition incapable of contributory negligence. For example, in Michigan, Illinois, North Carolina, Ohio, and Wisconsin, courts hold that children under seven are incapable of contributory negligence.* This means that even if such students contribute to their own injury by carelessness, they may be able to recover damages from a negligent school employee.

In addition, at least 13 states have comparative negligence statutes.** In these states, a high school student's negligence does not completely prevent her from recovering compensation even if that negligence played a part in producing her injury. Instead, the court or jury would compare the student's negligence with that of the school and would reduce the amount of compensation awarded to the student by the relative proportion of her negligence. However, many comparative negligence statutes bar recovery if the plaintiff's negligence is equal to or greater than the defendant's.[12]

Assumption of Risk. Since even a high degree of care may not prevent injury in some activities, the doctrine of "assumption of risk" has been recognized as a defense against liability. This means that students who voluntarily engage in certain activities, such as competitive sports, assume the normal and obvious risks that participation carries with it. The doctrine was successfully used by an Oregon high school in defending itself against a suit by a student who was severely injured when tackled by two players in a varsity football game.[13] Similarly, the doctrine might protect a

---

* In other states a child will not be conclusively presumed to be incapable of contributory negligence unless she is under 4 or 5 years.[10]

** As of 1976, the following states had passed comparative negligence statutes: Arkansas, Georgia, Hawaii, Maine, Massachusetts, Minnesota, Mississippi, Nebraska, New Hampshire, South Dakota, Wisconsin, Puerto Rico, and Washington.[11]

school against suit by a parent who is injured by a careless athlete or a foul ball while watching a sporting event from the sidelines. But it did not protect a coach who allowed a football player suffering from heat stroke to remain untreated for about two hours before calling a doctor.[14]

Governmental Immunity. In the past, most school districts were not held liable for the negligence of their employees under the common law theory that the state and its agencies were sovereign and could not be sued without their consent. Some courts defended this practice on the grounds that funds raised for schooling could not legally be diverted for non-educational purposes. But in recent years, the doctrine of governmental immunity has been almost unanimously condemned by legal writers and scholars, and it has been abolished in an increasing number of states. As the Pennsylvania Supreme Court recently wrote: "Whatever may have been the basis for the inception of the doctrine, it is clear that no public policy considerations presently justify its retention."[15]

By now, governmental immunity has been abolished in more than 50% of the states and has been modified in others by authorizing school districts to insure their staffs against possible negligence claims.*[16] But even in those states where schools can prevent negligence suits by asserting governmental immunity, parents may sue individual school employees, who still can be held personally liable for their negligence.

Parental Waivers. If a school requires parents to sign a waiver, release, or permission slip before allowing their children to undertake field trips or other unusual educational activities, are the teacher and the school automatically relieved of possible liability for negligence? No. Parents cannot waive their children's claim for damages. A teacher always has a duty to act with reasonable care, and a waiver does not change this duty. Moreover, a release given before liability arises may be meaningless, for some legal writers note that it is contrary to public policy to exempt a person or institution in advance from liability for its own negligence.[17]

---

* These states are: Alaska, Arizona, California, Colorado, Florida, Hawaii, Idaho, Iowa, Illinois, Indiana, Kentucky, Louisiana, Maine, Michigan, Minnesota, Nebraska, Nevada, New Jersey, New York, Oklahoma, Oregon, Pennsylvania, Rhode Island, Utah, Washington, Wisconsin, District of Columbia.

Can school employees be held liable for making false statements about students or parents?

It depends. Citizens cannot be sued for every false statement they make —only those that are defamatory. Defamation is a statement made about another person that is not true and that injures the person's reputation. Oral defamation is called slander; written defamation is called libel. A person can sue for libel without proving that he has suffered financial loss. But in most cases, a person who is slandered must prove that the false statements damaged him financially. Defamation requires that the damaging words be communicated to a third person; derogatory words directed at the plaintiff himself are no basis for legal action. And truth is a complete defense in any defamation suit.

When school officials make statements about students or parents that are required as part of their regular duties, they have a "qualified" or "limited privilege" which may be used as a defense against charges of libel or slander. This privilege may protect a school employee against liability for making a defamatory statement when the statement is made in good faith as part of his job. But if an educator makes a defamatory statement that he knows is false, or if he maliciously intends to damage a person's reputation, the qualified privilege is forfeited. And if school officials make false and damaging statements about students or parents outside the scope of their responsibilities—for example, in gossip to a neighbor or reporter or in a letter to a newspaper or friend—their qualified privilege does not protect them. Thus a California court held that school board members who mailed a public announcement accusing two students by name of "serious violation of manners, morals, and discipline" were not immune from a libel suit.[18]

Parents also have a qualified privilege in criticizing school employees through appropriate channels.[19] But they too may be held liable for defamation if they maliciously spread false information about teachers or administrators.[20]

Can school officials be held liable for violating a student's constitutional rights?

Yes. When two Arkansas students were unlawfully expelled without due process, their parents sued the school board for damages. Here the Supreme Court ruled that school officials could be held liable "if they knew or reasonably should have known that the action they took within their sphere of official responsibility would violate the constitutional rights of the students affected."[21] *

What if school officials were simply not aware of the student's rights?

The Court responded that an act violating a student's constitutional rights cannot be "justified by ignorance or disregard of settled, indisputable law on the part of one entrusted with supervision of students' daily lives." **

When will monetary damages be awarded?

When, as the Court ruled in this case, a school official has acted with a malicious intention "or with such disregard of the student's clearly established constitutional rights that his action cannot be reasonably be characterized as being in good faith."

---

* Such an improper action is becoming known as a "Constitutional tort."

** The Court noted that a school official must be held to a standard of conduct based not only on good intentions, "but also on knowledge of the basic, unquestioned constitutional rights of his charges."

Summary

In order to hold a school or its employees liable for injuring your child, you will have to prove three things:

(*1*) There was a breach of duty. Teachers have a duty to exercise reasonable care not to injure their students and to prevent injury to them. "Reasonable care" is that degree of care that a reasonable teacher of ordinary prudence would have exercised under the circumstances, which include the age, maturity, and experience of the pupils and the extent of the danger involved. When circumstances are more dangerous, as in shop or physical education, a reasonable teacher would be expected to be especially careful—to provide closer supervision, clear warnings, and careful instructions. If a school employee does not use reasonable care, there is a breach of duty, and she is negligent.

(*2*) The court must find that the breach of duty was the proximate or immediate cause of the injury. It is not enough to prove that a teacher failed to exercise reasonable care toward your injured son or daughter. You must also prove that this failure caused the injury.

(*3*) There was no contributory negligence. This means that if your child's own negligence contributed to his injury, if he failed to exercise that degree of care usually expected of a student of his age, knowledge, and experience, his carelessness may prevent recovery from a negligent teacher or administrator. However, the younger the student, the more difficult it is to prove contributory negligence. In the case of children under five or six, many courts will not even permit evidence of such negligence to be considered.

Other defenses against liability include assumption of risk and governmental immunity. Courts hold that students who voluntarily engage in activities such as competitive sports assume the normal risks of injury that go along with participation in these activities.

In some states, the doctrine of governmental immunity prevents parents from suing school districts for negligently injuring their children. But in recent decades, most states have abolished or modified this doctrine.

School employees can also be sued for libel or slander if they make false statements which injure the reputation of students or parents. Educators have a qualified privilege that might protect them against liability for defamatory statements made in good faith as part of their duties. But the privilege will not protect them from liability for false statements that are made maliciously or are made outside the scope of their responsibilities. In addition, school officials can be held liable for damages if they take actions which violate a student's clearly established constitutional rights.

In sum, the law requires persons who carelessly cause injury to pay compensation. School employees are subject to the same law as other citizens, who are held financially responsible for their negligence. However, since the law does not provide compensation for all student injuries, parents should consider protecting their children with medical insurance.

Chapter 9
Accountability and the Curriculum

Parents, educators, and judges generally agree that schools should be responsible for providing a sound education. But what should be done when the education is poor? Who then should be held accountable? And how should that accountability be enforced? Some parents believe that the best way is to use the law of torts, under which the victim of negligence can sue for money damages. According to this theory, if schools are negligent in teaching, they should be held financially liable for damages. Another view puts the emphasis on the students—advocating the use of required compe tency tests for students as a way to insure that minimum standards are met. This chapter discusses both of these approaches to accountability.

It also examines the issue of parental control over the curriculum, and considers such questions as: Should parent groups be able to demand new courses in the curriculum? Should they be able to prevent a school board from censoring library books? Do they have a right to object to specific courses or teaching materials that they find offensive? The chapter does not consider cases of individual parents objecting to texts or courses for their own children, since these objections are considered in the next chapter. It focuses on the rights of parents who object to having certain courses offered to *any* student.

Accountability

Can a school be held liable for poor instruction?

Probably not. In the fall of 1973, Peter W. Doe, a high school graduate with a fifth grade reading ability, sued the San Francisco School District for failing to provide him with adequate instruction in basic skills such as reading and writing.[1] Peter claimed that the school district negligently assigned him to classes with instructors unqualified to teach and classes not geared to his reading ability, failed to keep his parents advised concerning his educational problems, and allowed him to advance through the grades even though he did not achieve the knowledge required. His lawyer also argued that since schools and teachers have been held liable for failure to exercise reasonable care in situations that resulted in physical injury to students, there is no reason that their negligent teaching should be interpreted any differently. A California court disagreed.

Since schools had never before been held liable for negligent teaching, this case presented a question of public policy concerning the consequence of extending liability to educational malpractice. The court noted two problems that would have to be dealt with if liability was extended in this way. First, Peter Doe's alleged injuries would be difficult if not impossible for the courts to measure. "Classroom methodology," wrote the judge, "affords no readily acceptable standards of care, or cause, or injury." There are any number of conflicting educational theories about how or what a student should be taught. And professional authority indicates that the injury claimed in this case—the inability to read and write—is influenced "by a host of factors which affect the pupil subjectively, from outside the formal teaching process" and beyond the control of the schools. Thus the court found no objective and workable standard of care to measure the school's alleged misconduct and no way to determine a causal connection between the school's alleged negligence and the injury suffered.

Second, practical financial considerations also led to the rejection of Peter's claim. The court noted that in recent decades public schools have been charged with failure to achieve their educational objectives and with responsibility for many of society's problems. Under these circumstances, the court observed that "to hold them to an actionable 'duty of care' in the discharge of their academic functions, would expose them to the tort [negligence] claims—real or imagined—of disaffected students and parents in countless numbers." Since schools are already beset by so many problems, the ultimate consequence of permitting suits such as this "would burden them—and society—beyond calculation."

Related "Malpractice" Cases

Several related cases have recently come before the courts. In Long Island, New York, a 1976 high school graduate filed a five million dollar "educational malpractice" suit against his school district for allowing him to graduate despite the fact that he was functionally illiterate. The judge dismissed the suit because he could find no state precedent to support the legal action.[2] In March 1977, an Iowa judge ruled against 11 community college students who sought damages from the college for negligently hiring unqualified instructors and providing inadequate equipment. The judge refused "to expand the concept of negligence to include complaints arising from the area of academic education." [3] And in June 1977, a Connecticut judge ruled against a University of Bridgeport student who demanded her tuition back because her instructor did not teach what was promised in the college's course description. The judge indicated that an agreement to provide an education is different from other consumer services. "This is a contract which involves specialized, highly qualified talent and experts," he said, and the courts should stay away from cases that call upon them to decide what constitutes educational quality.[4] Thus, despite their widespread publicity, educational malpractice suits generally have been unsuccessful.

Who should be held accountable and how?

Because courts have not been willing to hold schools financially liable for negligent teaching, citizens have sought other means to hold schools accountable. While the concept of educational accountability is becoming increasingly popular, there is no general agreement about who should be held responsible for what or how. Many educators believe that teachers have too little control over all the factors that are involved in education to be held entirely responsible, and some propose the concept of "joint accountability," in which criteria would be established to define the responsibilities and measure the effectiveness of parents, administrators and pupil personnel services as well as teachers and students. While many educators agree with this idea, schools generally have not been able to implement it effectively.

Competency:

One concrete result of citizen concern for accountability has been the recent and rapid expansion of minimum competency testing for high school graduation and grade-to-grade promotion.

What states have competency requirements?

By June 1, 1977, twenty-four states had taken action on this subject, nine through legislation (California, Colorado, Florida, Maryland, New Jersey, Nevada, Virginia, Washington, and Louisiana), and fifteen through state board of education rulings (Arizona, Delaware, Georgia, Idaho, Kentucky, Michigan, Missouri, Nebraska, New Hampshire, New Mexico, New York, Oklahoma, Oregon, Rhode Island and Vermont).[5] And in a number of other states, legislation is now pending.

Typical statutes require that the state board or local districts establish standards of proficiency in basic skills such as reading, writing, and computation and that students be tested periodically (e.g., in the 7th, 9th, 11th and 12th grades). Regulations often provide for parent conferences and remedial instruction for those who fail to demonstrate the prescribed competencies. Advocates of this approach believe that if competency testing is implemented appropriately, schools will eliminate the misunderstandings that gave rise to the Peter Doe case.

The Curriculum

Do parent groups have the right to control school policy and curriculum?

No. The U.S. Constitution puts the states in charge of education. State legislatures typically make broad pronouncements concerning educational goals and programs and then delegate to state boards of education and local districts the carrying out of these programs and goals. Usually the local school board has primary authority and responsibility for hiring and firing teachers and administrators; establishing priorities; choosing texts and resolving educational disputes among competing groups of parents, teachers, and students. As the Supreme Court has written: "By and large public education in our nation is committed to the control of state and local authorities. Courts do not and cannot intervene in the resolution of conflicts which arise in the daily operation of school systems and which do not directly and sharply implicate basic constitutional values." [6] Thus if parent groups are dissatisfied with a school's policy, curriculum, or staff, they usually will have to try to persuade school boards or legislatures to make the changes they advocate or persuade the courts that their position is based on statutory or constitutional grounds.

Do parents have the right to participate in the development of school policy?

Federal law and local school board regulation are increasingly encouraging parents to participate in planning school policy. All parents can share their concerns and suggestions with the school board members who represent them. In addition, they have the right to attend school board meetings. Under federal statute, parents whose children are defined as educationally deprived have the right to participate in parent councils which must be consulted by school officials in planning and carrying out programs that affect their children.* And the parents of handicapped children have the right to participate in the development of individual educational plans for their children.**

Do parents have the right to object to specific books or materials?

Parents have objected to a variety of curricular materials on grounds that they violated their religious beliefs, that they were obscene and contained dirty words, that they taught prejudicial attitudes, and that they dealt with topics which they did not believe should be part of the school curriculum—sex education, for example. Here are the ways some courts have dealt with these issues.

Compulsory Sex Education. In Baltimore, a group of parents sued the Maryland Board of Education to prevent it from implementing its regulation requiring all local school systems to provide "a comprehensive program of family life and sex education in every elementary and secondary school for all students" as an integral part of the health education curriculum.[7] The parents claimed that they had "the exclusive constitutional right to teach their children about sexual matters in their own homes" and that this right should prohibit the schools from teaching about sex. The court disagreed. It held that the requirement was a reasonable public health measure, that it raised no significant constitutional questions, and that in this case the state's interest in the health of its children outweighed the parents' claim.

Informal Pressure. In a related California case, a parents' organization, Citizens for Parental Rights, brought suit to prevent the teaching of family life and sex education courses in five school districts.[8] The parents argued that the program violated their religious beliefs and would expose their children to certain subjects that were sinful. Although state law allowed

---

* This subject is further discussed in Chapter 13.

** The subject is further discussed in Chapter 12.

parents to keep their children from participating in the program, the parents argued that there was a strong informal pressure on the students to attend, and this pressure interfered with their religious freedom. But the court did not believe this social pressure amounted to a violation of the constitutional rights of the parents or their children. It noted that "a mere personal difference of opinion as to the curriculum which is taught in our public school system does not give rise to a constitutional right in the private citizen to control exposure to knowledge."

Further, the court pointed out that if a judge prohibited the sex education program because it offended the religious beliefs of certain parents, he would be violating the First Amendment, which prohibits the state from tailoring its curriculum in accord with the principles or dogmas of any religion. Such an approach would permit any group of parents "to create chaos in the school system" by attempting to prohibit portions of the curriculum that were contrary to their beliefs.

Offensive Anti-Religious Texts. During the 1974-75 school term, an intense and sometimes violent controversy arose in Kanawha County, West Virginia following the adoption of a series of textbooks for the county's public school system,[9] and some parents who objected to the texts took their case to court. They argued that the books should be removed because they contained matter that is "offensive to Christian morals . . . defames the Nation . . . encourages the use of vile and abusive language," and encourages violation of both the Ten Commandments and civil law. After considering the parents' testimony, the court concluded that some of the controversial materials were indeed "offensive to plaintiff's beliefs, choices of language, and code of conduct." Nevertheless, the court did not find that placing these texts in the county schools violated any of the parents' constitutional rights. Judge Hall observed that freedom of religion "does not guarantee that nothing about religion will be taught in the schools nor that nothing offensive to any religion will be taught." Instead, the Constitution prohibits states from encouraging or discouraging any religion, and it requires them to be neutral between different religions and between religion and non-religion. In conclusion, the judge emphasized that where no constitutional violations are involved, parents who object to texts should not go to court but should pursue their concerns "through board of education proceedings or ultimately at the polls on election day."

Dirty Words and Obscene Books. Robert Keefe was a high school English teacher who assigned his senior class an article from *The Atlantic* entitled "The Young and the Old" which discussed dissent, protest, and revolt.[10] The article repeatedly contained the word "motherfucker." A number of parents found the word highly offensive and protested to the school committee. Because of the protests, Keefe was suspended when he refused to agree never to use the word again in class. But a federal court ruled that Keefe's suspension violated his constitutional rights, and concluded that the sensibilities of offended parents "are not the full measure of what is proper in education." It also commented on these questions:

Isn't an article that repeatedly uses vulgar words improper?

It depends on the article. The judge found the article in this case to be a scholarly, thoughtful and thought-provoking piece which in no way suggested immoral conduct.

Can't a school committee protect students from language that the parents of some students find genuinely offensive?

This would depend on the specific situation—the age of the students, the words used, and the purpose in which they were used. In this instance, most high school seniors knew the word, it was used for valid educational purposes and its use caused no classroom disruption.

Can a teacher assign any book that is published? Are obscenity standards the same for students as for adults?

No. The issue is one of degree and depends on the circumstances of each case. The court's concern for safeguarding academic freedom protected Keefe because of the quality, relevance and purpose of his assignment. Academic freedom is based on the First Amendment and the need in a democracy to protect the right of teachers and students to challenge established concepts and thus allow for social progress. But the First Amendment does not protect obscenity.

When are books obscene for students?

According to current Supreme Court standards, a book is obscene if it "appeals to the prurient interest" of minors, describes sexual conduct "in a patently offensive way," and "lacks serious literary, artistic, political or scientific value."[11] To apply these tests, the material must be judged "as a whole" and by "contemporary community standards."

In a 1974 Ohio case, a state court ruled that Claude Brown's *Manchild in the Promised Land* and Ken Kesey's *One Flew Over the Cuckoo's Nest* violated all these standards. The books were assigned reading in two optional high school courses and were objected to by a group of parents. The court agreed with the parents that "each of these books is offensive to prevailing standards in the adult community with respect to what is suitable for juveniles." While it prohibited the school from assigning them as part of the curriculum, it allowed them to be used where a parent "has knowledge of the character of the books and consents to their use." [12]

Derogatory Materials. In New York City, two parents asked a court to prevent the schools from using *Oliver Twist* by Charles Dickens and *The Merchant of Venice* by William Shakespeare because of their anti-Jewish bias.[13] The court refused. It wrote: "If evaluation of any literary work is permitted to be based upon a requirement that each book be free from derogatory reference to any religion, race, country, nation, or personality, endless litigation respecting many books would probably ensue . . ." The court concluded that it would be wrong to interfere with the discretion of school officials to assign these books since the officials acted in good faith and without malice or prejudice."

Do parents have the right to prevent a school committee from censoring curriculum materials or library books?

They probably do. In 1976, a federal appeals court ruled that an Ohio school committee did not have the right to remove books from the library because its members found them objectionable.[14] The case arose in a Cleveland suburb when the school committee voted to remove Kurt Vonnegut's *Cat's Cradle* and *God Bless You, Mr. Rosewater* and Joseph Heller's *Catch 22* from all school libraries.

The court acknowledged that local school boards had authority to select and purchase text books over the objection of parent or teacher groups. Further, the judge noted that a school board is under no obligation to provide a library at any school or to choose any particular books. However, once a board creates a library, it cannot place conditions on the use of the library that are "related solely to the social or political tastes of school board members," and therefore the board could not remove books because it found them objectionable in content and because it felt it had power "to censor the school library for subject matter which the board members found distasteful." The court declared these actions unconstitutional, and ordered the library books replaced.

On the other hand, a different federal court upheld the right of a New York school board to remove Piri Thomas' *Down These Mean Streets* from its junior high school libraries.[15] The action of the board was taken as a result of parent pressures, and a compromise allowed the book to remain in the schools and to be made available to the parents of students who requested it. In its decision the court wrote: "It is predictable that no matter what choice of books may be made by whatever segment of academe, some other person or group may well dissent." Therefore, it ruled that shelving or unshelving of books does not present a constitutional issue, "particularly where there is no showing of a curtailment of freedom of speech or thought."

Do parent groups have the right to demand that specific courses be added to the curriculum?

Generally not—except through school board procedures that allow citizens to petition the board concerning educational matters. However, Massachusetts and Rhode Island have statutes that specifically allow a certain number of parents to request new courses.* For example, the Massachusetts law provides that any course not included in the public high school curriculum shall be taught if parents of 20 pupils request such a course in writing and there is a qualified teacher available.

---

* The Massachusetts law applies to high schools with more than 150 students, and provides that such courses receive the same academic credit as regular courses.[16] The Rhode Island law provides that when 20 students apply for a course in Portuguese, Italian or Spanish, the school committee shall arrange that such a course be given by a competent teacher.[17]

Summary

Although courts hold school officials liable if their negligence results in a physical injury to students, judges have not been willing to allow parents to collect damages from schools for negligent teaching. This is one reason citizens concerned about educational responsibility have turned to state legislatures and boards of education in their efforts to hold schools accountable. In recent years, in an effort to improve standards and promote accountability, 24 states have passed laws or issued regulations calling for minimum competency testing for high school graduation and grade-to-grade promotion.

Parent groups have also gone to court to force the schools to change features of the curriculum they found objectionable. They have asserted the right to prohibit courses on family life and sex education, to remove texts that offended their religious beliefs or moral values, and to prohibit books that used dirty or vulgar language. But judges generally have been unwilling to force schools to comply with these demands. Since school officials have been delegated the responsibility of making educational decisions, courts are unwilling to substitute their judgment for the judgment of professional educators in such matters—except where a valid constitutional objection is made.

If school officials violate the constitutional rights of students or parents, the courts will act to protect those rights. But if parents disagree with the educational decisions that administrators make, the courts urge them to use school board procedures or political and legislative action rather than the courts to create change.

Although school boards have wide authority, board members cannot use their power to censor books because they find them personally objectionable. And while parent groups cannot object to the use of books merely because they contain vulgar language, schools have no right to assign to minors books that are legally obscene.

In sum, the courts are reluctant to allow any group of parents to control the texts, courses, or curriculum for all students. But, as the next chapter will indicate, they are more sympathetic to parents who assert their right to control the education of their own children.

Chapter 10
The Right to Guide

The U.S. Supreme Court has clearly held that parents have the right "to guide the education of their children." But the state also has a legitimate interest in the schooling of its future citizens, and it can therefore compel parents to provide their children with an adequate education. When school officials and parents disagree about what is best for youngsters, the rights of parents may collide with those of the state. This chapter considers how some of these conflicts are resolved and examines such questions as: Can states require that all children attend a public school? Can parents withdraw their children from school when it is dangerous or because of objectionable courses? If so, do parents have the right to educate their children at home? Unlike most legal issues considered in this book, many of the answers to these questions depend on specific state statutes and local judicial interpretations.

Can states require all students to attend public schools?

No. As we pointed out in Chapter 4, parents have the right to send their children to private schools, either religious or secular. This right was established by the Supreme Court more than 50 years ago in a case involving a state statute which required all parents to send their children to public school until age 16.[1] In holding the statute unconstitutional, the Court ruled that the state may not unreasonably interfere with "the liberty of parents and guardians to direct the upbringing and education of children under their control." A "child is not the mere creature of the state," the Court said, and the state has no right "to standardize its children by forcing them to accept instruction by public teachers only."

Although states cannot compel parents to send their children to public schools, courts have consistently held that they *can* compel parents to send their children to school. This was reaffirmed in a recent federal case in which two Chicago parents claimed that the state compulsory education law violated their constitutional right to educate their children "as they see fit" and "in accordance with their determination of what best serves the family's interest." [2] In this case, the court ruled that the parents had failed to show any "fundamental right which has been abridged by the compulsory attendance statute." The judge pointed out that the parents' constitutional right to guide their children's education is a limited one; "it merely provides parents with an opportunity to seek a reasonable alternative to public education."

Can states regulate private schools?

Yes, states can establish minimum standards for private schools. In 1968, the Supreme Court wrote that the state has a "proper interest in the manner in which those schools perform their secular educational function." [3] The Court noted that states have power "to insist that attendance at private schools, if it is to satisfy state compulsory attendance laws, be at institutions which provide minimum hours of instruction, employ teachers of specified training, and cover prescribed subjects of instruction."

But state standards may be held unconstitutional if they go too far in controlling private education. For example, in a recent Ohio case parents objected to detailed "minimum standards" that regulated not only hours of instruction and teacher qualifications but also curriculum content, teaching methods, the physical layout of the building, and educational policies.[4] The court wrote that these standards were "so pervasive and all-encompassing" that total compliance with each standard by a private school "would effectively eradicate the distinction between public and non-public education" and thereby deprive the parents of their right to direct the education of their children.

Do parents have the right to educate their children at home?

The answer depends on the wording of the state education statute and the local court's interpretation of what constitutes a "school." Here are a few examples of the different ways the courts have ruled in different states.

The Levisen Case, a liberal interpretation.[5] In Illinois, the parents of a seven year old girl were convicted of violating the state's compulsory attendance law. They appealed. The evidence indicated that the mother had been teaching her daughter at home for five hours a day and that the child showed "proficiency comparable with average third-grade students." Her college-educated parents did not send her to school because they believed that for a child's first 8 or 10 years "the mother is the best teacher" and that education in competition with other students "produces a pugnacious character."

The Illinois law required parents to send children between the age of seven and 16 to public schools, but exempted children attending "a private or parochial school where children are taught the branches of education taught to children of corresponding age and grade in public schools." Since the Levisens provided comparable instruction for their daughter, they contended that she was attending a "private school" within the meaning of the law. The Supreme Court of Illinois agreed.

The court noted that compulsory education laws were enacted "to enforce the natural obligation of parents" to educate their children. "The object," wrote the court, "is that all children shall be educated, not that they shall be educated in any particular manner or place." Since the Levisen child was taught third-grade subjects, had regular hours of study, had third-grade proficiency and was not educationally neglected, the court ruled that the term "private school" covered the "place and nature of instruction" provided in this case. The judge emphasized that no parent had a right to deprive his child of educational advantages at least comparable with school board standards. But he concluded: "The law is not made to punish those who provide their children with instruction equal or superior to that obtainable in the public schools. It is made for the parent who fails or refuses to properly educate his child." *

A Strict Interpretation: The O'Brien Case.[7] The O'Briens took two of their children out of a New Jersey elementary school to educate them at home. Although their mother held a bachelor's degree in education, a state court ruled that her children did not receive instruction equivalent to that provided in the public schools. According to the court, "equivalent" instruction required: (*1*) that standard, approved teaching materials be used; (*2*) that the instructor possess the necessary qualifications; and (*3*) that the children have the full advantages supplied by the public schools.

While the judge found that the teaching materials used by the O'Briens

---

* And in a recent New York case, the judge wrote: "It is settled law that a parent need not avail himself of formal educational facilities for a child in order to satisfy the requirements of the law, it being sufficient that a systematic course of study be undertaken at home and that the parent render qualified, quality instruction." [6]

were adequate, he held that their home instruction failed to meet the other two criteria. Because Mrs. O'Brien had been certified to teach in secondary schools only and had not kept up with educational developments during the 20 years since she had taught, the court ruled that her qualifications were not equivalent to those required of local public elementary school teachers. The O'Brien children's lack of opportunity to associate and play with other children of their age was a second factor that led the court to conclude they were not receiving an equivalent education.

Despite the *O'Brien* decision, a subsequent New Jersey court focused on parental teaching ability rather than formal education and also doubted that state law required "equivalent social contact." [8] But other states continue to emphasize parental qualifications. The Supreme Court of Washington, for example, ruled that a home instruction program did not meet state standards solely because the parents did not hold a valid state teacher's certificate or diploma.[9] California, like several other states, recognizes the right of parents to educate their children themselves or by private tutor, but only if the parents or tutor hold a "valid state credential for the grade taught." [10] *

Thus some states, such as Washington and California, require parents to have formal teaching qualifications to satisfy their compulsory education requirements. But others, such as New York and Illinois, focus on the quality and standard of instruction rather than the credentials of the instructor.

Can parents withdraw their children from specific courses?

Older decisions say yes. In an 1891 case, for example, a father demanded that his daughter be excused from studying grammar because he objected to the way it was taught.[12] The question, said the court, is who should determine what a child should study, "a teacher who has a mere temporary interest in her welfare, or her father who may reasonably be supposed to be desirous of pursuing such course as will best promote the happiness of his child?" The court ruled that the parent has "a right to make a reasonable selection from the prescribed studies for his child," and this selection must be respected by the school. According to the court, any rule compelling a child to take a course contrary to the wishes of her parent is "arbitrary and unreasonable."

---

* A New York court recently ruled that the state's compulsory education law was not met by instruction at home for one and a half hours a day by a mother whose formal education ceased after her high school graduation.[11]

In a subsequent Nebraska case, a father wanted his 12-year-old daughter to skip her last required class in domestic science and take private music lessons instead.[13] The school refused, on the grounds that allowing any exceptions to required courses would disrupt discipline. The judge did not agree. He could not see that excusing the student from a cooking class "could have interfered with the discipline of the school." In any event, he ruled that "the parent has a right" to make this decision.

Tests and Criteria

The above cases indicate that parents can sometimes withdraw their children from specific courses. The following decisions consider some of the tests or criteria courts have used to decide when such parental decisions should be upheld.

Essential for Citizenship. In a 1927 case concerning Bible reading, the Supreme Court of Colorado indicated that "children cannot be compelled to take instruction not essential to good citizenship." [14] The school board had argued that if parents object to required subjects, they should send their children to private institutions. The judges rejected this argument because it would force a parent "to surrender his rights in the public schools." The school board's "control over instruction," wrote the court, does not mean that "every child should be required to take every subject which the board puts on the list." However, the school can require "studies plainly essential to good citizenship."

How could this test be applied today? What knowledge is essential to enable children to fulfill the social and political responsibilities of citizenship? Different parents, school boards and judges might answer this question differently. But the Deputy Attorney General of California recently supported the "good citizenship" standard and illustrated how it might be applied. Under this test, he wrote, "elementary mathematics could be required, although calculus could not; handwriting could be required, creative writing could not." In any event, he noted that "when the state chooses to override a parent's wish, the burden is on the state to establish that in order to function effectively as a citizen one must be versed in the subject to which the parent objects." [15]

Religion and Conscience. In 1921, a California court considered whether children of parents opposed to dancing can be compelled to participate when such activities are part of a school physical education program.[16] The school authorities argued that their dance program did not violate any established religious doctrine. In response, the court commented that religious reasons were not the only basis for legitimate parental objection. It can also be a "question of morals which may concern the conscience of those who are not affiliated with any particular religious sect."

In ruling in favor of these parents, the court wrote that this involves:

> "... The right of parents to control their own children—to require them to live up to the teachings and the principles which are inculcated in them at home under the parental authority.... Has the state the right to enact a law ... the effect of which would be to alienate in a measure the children from parental authority?.... To answer ... in the affirmative would be to give sanction to a power over home life that might result in denying parents their natural as well as their constitutional rights to govern, within the scope of just parental authority, their own progeny."

A more recent New Jersey case concerned parents who raised religious objections to their children being required to take a compulsory course entitled "Human Sexuality." [17] The school board's evidence indicated that 70% of the local citizens believed that sex education courses were "necessary and beneficial for the students." But the court noted that this was not an issue to be decided by majority vote. "If majority vote were to govern in matters of religion and conscience," wrote the judge, "there would be no need for the First Amendment," which was adopted to protect the one percent or one person "who is sincere in a conscientious religious conviction." In conclusion, the court noted that if educators are not careful about what they compel, parental discipline and respect will diminish "as the great sovereign state forces its way into the home as a foster parent."

Do parents have the right to remove their children from a school that is not safe?

Yes. According to the Supreme Court of Pennsylvania, "a parent is justified in withdrawing his child from a school where the health and welfare of the child is threatened." [18]

What conditions are threatening enough to override compulsory education laws?

This is a matter of interpretation. In the Pennsylvania case, the court did not support the right of a group of parents to withdraw their 47 children from a school to which they had been recently assigned to improve racial balance and reduce overcrowding. Despite evidence of harassment, the court noted that these incidents only applied to 11 of the 47 students and that after the harassment, officials had taken steps to improve the safety of the school.

In a more recent case, Earl and Jane Ross were convicted of violating a state compulsory attendance law for failing to allow their two children to be bused to vocational training classes one day a week.[19] The parents claimed that the vocational school was unsafe, and they cited two "unpleasant experiences" to support their claim. In 1975, a state appeals court ruled that the two incidents "were not such threats to the health and safety of the Ross children as to justify the action of their parents." The court concluded that the state education law "does not authorize parents to withdraw their children from classes and activities except where the children's health and safety are positively and immediately threatened."

On the other hand, a New York court allowed parents to remove their two daughters from one elementary school and place them in another over school board objections because they had been beaten at the school to which they were assigned.[20]

Summary

Although state compulsory education laws have been consistently upheld by the courts, parents have the right to send their children to a public or private school. And if they choose a non-public school, they can select a religious or non-sectarian institution. Such private schools can be regulated by the state which can set minimum standards for instruction and teacher qualification. But these standards cannot be so detailed and pervasive that they would effectively abolish the distinction between public and private education.

The right of parents to educate their children at home and to withdraw them from specific courses depends on state law. There are some statutes and court decisions that specifically allow parents to educate their children at home if the instruction is "equivalent" to that which is provided in public or approved private schools. In some states, this is allowed only if such parents are certified teachers and use approved texts. An alternative approach suggested by some courts is to focus on a student's achievement in standard subjects: home instruction is "equivalent" if the child's progress is as good as the norm in the local public schools. While this approach seems objective and could eliminate questions of parental credentials, it necessarily relies on the use of standardized tests, and these usually fail to account for individual differences.

Early cases indicated that parents had a right to excuse their children from any course offered by the schools. Today, however, schools can generally compel students to attend courses that are deemed "basic" or "essential for good citizenship"—even over the objections of parents. But if parents can show that a course clearly violates their religious freedom, such objections will have a better chance of being respected by the courts. And several states (e.g., California, Michigan, Idaho, and New Mexico) have legislation that authorizes parents to excuse their children from specific courses such as sex education and family life instruction.[21] Finally, parents clearly have the right to withdraw their children from an unsafe school where their health and welfare is seriously threatened.

Chapter 11
Student Records: The Right of Privacy and The Right to Know

In 1925, the National Education Association recommended that schools maintain health, guidance, and psychological records on each pupil, so that information would be available about the "whole child," not just his grades and the subjects he studied. At the time, the proposal was generally viewed as progressive.

In subsequent years many school districts developed elaborate records on each student. In New York City, for example, student records typically included a card on personal and social behavior; teachers' recommendations for tracking; a guidance record of counselor's evaluations of aptitude, behavior and personality characteristics; all disciplinary referral cards; and a teacher's anecdotal file on student behavior—all these in addition to cards containing standardized test results, grades and health information.[1] These records were open to government investigators, employers, and other non-school personnel. But they were not open to parents.

As the quality of information grew so did the abuses. As a result, a number of state and local governments passed laws that opened school records to parents. Then, in 1974, Congress passed the Family Educational Rights and Privacy Act, which provides such access to every parent in every state. This chapter will outline some of the problems that led to this legislation and then will explain the key features of the Act: the parents' right to know, limited access by outsiders, and the right to challenge and correct misleading information.

Problems and Abuses. Over the years, many cases of the misuse of school records came to light. A mother, for example, was told she had no right to see the records that resulted in her son being transferred to a class for the mentally retarded. A father, attending a routine parent-teacher conference, discovered in his son's record such comments by teachers as that he was "strangely introspective" in the third grade, "unnaturally interested in girls" in the fifth, and had developed "peculiar political ideas" by the time he was 12.[2] Another parent found that the principal of his son's high school had inserted in the boy's record the principal's critique of a radio speech the youngster had given.[3] By the 1960's, researchers found that the CIA and the FBI had complete access to student files in more than 60% of school districts, while parents had access in only about 15%.[4]

As a result of cases such as these, some parents went to court. In 1961, for example, Edward Van Allen was told by teachers that his son needed psychological treatment, but was refused permission to see all of the boy's school records. Therefore, Van Allen took his case to a New York court which ruled that parents were entitled to inspect their children's school records.[5]

Other parents helped promote state and local regulations to control misuse of student records and during the 1960's many states enacted legislation on the subject. But very few were comprehensive. They tended to deal with only some of the problems, and the resolution of uncertainties was left to the discretion of local officials. In a number of states there were no statutes or regulations at all.[6]

A National Report. In 1969, a group of prominent educators and lawyers was convened by the Russell Sage Foundation to consider the ethical and legal aspects of school record keeping. The conferees found that school practices concerning the collection and use of information about pupils "threaten a desirable balance between the individual's right to privacy and the school's stated need to know,"[7] and noted these problems:

- Information about both pupils and their parents is often collected without the informed consent of either children or parents.
- Pupils and their parents typically have little knowledge of what information about them is contained in school records or of how it is used.
- Parental and pupil access to school records is typically limited by schools to attendance and achievement records.
- The secrecy with which school records are usually maintained makes it difficult for parents to assess their accuracy. Since formal procedures for challenging erroneous information generally do not exist, an unverified allegation of misconduct may become a part of a student's permanent record.
- Few provisions are made to protect school records from examination by unauthorized people.

- Formal policies for regulating access to records by non-school personnel do not exist in most school systems.

The report concluded that these deficiencies in record keeping "constitute a serious threat to individual privacy in the United States." Because of problems such as these and the lack of uniform or comprenensive state regulation, national legislation was needed.

Federal Legislation. The Family Educational Rights and Privacy Act (also known as the Buckley Amendment) was passed by Congress in 1974.[8] It established national minimum rights and standards concerning the use of school records. The Act contains several important features. It guarantees parents or guardians the right to inspect their child's records; it protects the confidentiality of student records; and it provides procedures through which parents can challenge questionable recorded information. The Act applies to all schools receiving federal education money and to any student who attends or has attended such a school. Students' rights may be asserted by their parents until they become 18 (or begin attending a postsecondary institution) at which time the students acquire the rights on their own.

The Right to Know. The Act states that no federal funds will be made available to any school which prevents parents from exercising "the right to inspect and review the education records of their children." These inspection rights include the right: (*1*) to be informed about the types and location of education records maintained by the school and the officials responsible for them; (*2*) to obtain copies of the records at a price not greater than the cost of reproducing them; and (*3*) to receive an explanation or interpretation of the records if requested. To facilitate the exercise of these rights, schools are required to inform eligible students and parents at least once every year of the requirements of the Act and the school's procedures for carrying them out.*

Confidentiality and Limited Access. The Act provides that a student's education records are not to be released by the school to any individual, agency, or organization without the parents' written consent, and that the consent applies only to the specific groups of individuals it mentions. There are a few limited exceptions, including officials of the same school who have a "legitimate educational interest," officials of other schools to which the

---

* See Appendix D for an example of the way one school district has met this requirement.

student has applied (provided the parents are notified), and persons for whom the information is necessary in an emergency "to protect the health or safety" of the student or others. In addition, the school must keep a file of all requests for access to a student's record and this information must be kept with the student's education records and must indicate the grounds on which access was granted.

Challenge and Hearing. The Act requires schools to provide parents with the right to challenge recorded information that is "inaccurate, misleading, or otherwise in violation of the privacy or other rights of students." A parent who believes that his child's record contains improper information may request that the records be amended. If the school refuses, it must inform the parents within a reasonable time and advise them of their right to a hearing.

Federal regulations specify minimum due process for such a hearing: (*1*) it must be held within a reasonable time following a request; (*2*) a written decision must be rendered by a school official or other person "who does not have a direct interest in the outcome of the hearing;" (*3*) parents must be given "a full and fair opportunity to present evidence;" and (*4*) parents may at their own expense be assisted or represented by any individual of their choice, including an attorney.

If, as a result of the hearing, the school decides that the information is inaccurate or misleading, it must amend the student's record accordingly and so inform the parent. If the school decides the information does not violate the student's rights it must inform the parents of "the right to place in the education records of the student a statement commenting upon the information . . . and/or setting forth any reasons for disagreeing with the decision" of the school. Such explanations must be maintained by the school as part of the student's record; and if the contested portion of the record is disclosed to anyone, the explanation must also be disclosed at the same time.

Other Provisions. Generally, either parent has the authority to exercise the rights contained in the Act. And divorce does not change these rights. The Act applies to past as well as current students, although former students and parents need not be notified annually about their rights under the law. If state law does not determine how long student records must be kept, they may be destroyed at the discretion of the school except when there is an outstanding request to inspect them. Unless parents object, a school may freely disclose such "directory information" as a student's name, address, birthdate, field of study, and team memberships. Students applying for admission to post-secondary schools may waive their right to see confidential recommendations. Moreover, the schools to which they apply do not have to give the students access to their parents' financial statements or records.

What can parents do if their rights are violated?

A special office has been established in Washington, D.C. to investigate violations of the Act.* When parents feel their rights are violated, they can file written complaints "within 180 days of the act or omission complained of." After receiving a parental complaint, the Office is required to notify the school of the alleged violation, to investigate, and to notify the parent and school of the results of its investigation. If a violation is found, the school will be told what it must do to comply. If the school does not comply, a Review Board hearing is held and if the Review Board rules against the school, its federal funding is cut off.

* To file a complaint or to seek further information about the Act, parents should write to: Fair Information Practice, Department of Health, Education and Welfare, 200 Independence Avenue, S.W., Washington, D.C. 20201.

Summary

Abuses in the use of student records led Congress to pass the Family Educational Rights and Privacy Act of 1974. The Act has several important features of interest to all parents. First, it guarantees parents the right to inspect and review their children's education records. Second, it strictly limits access to student records. With a few exceptions, it provides that these records are not to be released to any individual or organization without the parents' written consent. Third, it gives parents the right to challenge recorded information that is "inaccurate, misleading or otherwise in violation of the privacy or other rights of students." It also grants minimum procedural rights to any parents who wish to challenge the information in their children's records and gives them the right to place an explanation in the record of any information with which they disagree. In addition, the Act contains procedures for notifying parents of its provisions, and outlines what parents can do if their rights are violated. Thus the Act marks an important new advance in parents' rights.

Chapter 12
Special Education

Until quite recently most states with compulsory education laws also provided legal ways to exclude some children from school. Various labels were attached to the children who were excluded, but in general they were lumped together under the heading of "uneducable." Throughout the country hundreds of thousands of children were excluded from public schools on the basis of such laws. While in the past many parents and educators expected very little of these children and accepted the belief that most of them were uneducable and untrainable, a very different view is generally held today. According to this newer idea, *all* human beings can benefit from appropriate education or training. It is now established that with proper care, education and training, most handicapped children can learn enough to become largely self-sufficient and even the extreme cases can be trained to care for their own bodily needs. Very few need to remain completely dependent on the care of others.

The first case to reflect this changing view reached the courts in 1972, when the parents of 13 retarded children, together with the Pennsylvania Association for Retarded Children, challenged the laws in their state that kept children from school if they were certified by school psychologists as "uneducable and untrainable." [1] The parents claimed that the laws were unconstitutional: (*a*) by not giving parents a notice and proper hearing, they violated the right to due process; (*b*) by assuming certain children to be uneducable without a rational basis in fact, they denied the right to equal protection of the laws and; (*c*) because the state constitution guaranteed education for all children, the laws that excluded retarded children were arbitrary and capricious.

In this chapter we consider some important cases and recent legislation that dramatically affected parents' and students' rights in the area of special education. We first examine some cases that extended the right to education to all children, including the handicapped. Next we present the key features of a recently enacted federal law that provides both for parent participation and for due process in the identification and school or class placement of handicapped children.

May states deny schooling to retarded children?

In the Pennsylvania (PARC) case described above, the court said no and gave the contending parties the responsibility of working out an acceptable settlement. They came to an agreement which makes careful and elaborate provisions for due process before any child may be placed in special education classes or before any change in such placement may be made.

Some mentally retarded children might be most appropriately placed in special classes. But some normal children, too, may be placed in such classes because they have been misdiagnosed.* An important function of due process is to reduce the risk of such mistakes in diagnosis and educational placement.

In approving this agreement, the court pointed out that placing the label "retarded" on a child and placing him in a class for the retarded, itself creates a handicap, and that it is therefore important to guard against an inappropriate educational placement. The agreement also stipulated that state laws may not exclude mentally retarded children from a free program of public education, but must provide such a program for them. The least desirable way of educating the mentally retarded, the agreement said, was through homebound instruction, which could be used only when qualified educators judged it to be the most appropriate procedure for a particular child. And where such an arrangement is made, it must be re-evaluated every three months, with notice to the parent or guardian, who may request a hearing on the case.

Further, while rejecting in principle the idea that some children are completely incapable of education or training, the two parties agreed that some children are "uneducable and untrainable" in the public schools, and the agreement provided that the education of these children should come under the jurisdiction of the Department of Public Welfare.

---

* A number of factors could lead to a misdiagnosis: the child might come from a non-English speaking home, might have a perceptual difficulty, might be placed in a poor testing situation, might be culturally deprived, or ill on the day of testing.

May schools exclude the emotionally disturbed, the deaf, blind, or other "disabled" children?

A federal court in Washington, D.C. responded with a firm *no* to this question,[2] in a case which goes beyond the provisions of the Pennsylvania case by including not merely mental retardation but all types of handicap.

As in Pennsylvania, the facts showed that thousands of "exceptional" * children in Washington, D.C. were being excluded from school even though local laws provided mandatory free public education for all children between the ages of seven and sixteen. The District court ruled that the constitutional right of due process must be followed before any child is identified as "exceptional" and before an educational placement is decided upon for such a child.

The court further ruled that lack of funds for identifying and educating "exceptional" children could not be used as an excuse for failing to provide them with appropriate education. If funds are inadequate, they must nevertheless be used for *all* children equally. No child, said the court, should be completely excluded from publicly supported education:

> "The inadequacies of the District of Columbia Public School System, whether occasioned by insufficient funding or administrative inefficiency, certainly cannot be permitted to bear more heavily on the 'exceptional' or handicapped child than on the normal child."

In sum, the court ruled in favor of the parents of "exceptional" children on due process and equal protection grounds. The ruling included an elaborate set of procedures through which parents would be informed and involved every step of the way in working with the schools toward an appropriate educational placement of their children.

These cases, together with others in various parts of the country, made it clear that the right to education provided by the state extends to *all* children, including the handicapped. Beyond this basic right, however, other issues concerning the handicapped arose and were settled in the courts or by statutes. Among them were questions related to the proper placement of exceptional children—whether they should be placed in separate classes and schools or placed together with other students. Furthermore, what are

---

* Exceptional" children included the mentally retarded, emotionally disturbed, physically handicapped, hyperactive and other children with behavioral problems. The court refers to an estimate that in 1972 as many as 18,000 of these children were not being furnished programs in Washington, D.C.

the proper procedures by which to make such decisions, and what role, if any, should parents have in these procedures?

Related Cases In Other States

Since it has now been shown that many "exceptional" children will succeed in ordinary classrooms, particularly if their teachers receive some support services from trained specialists, large numbers of these children are now being "mainstreamed" in many states.

Children with significant disabilities may still be segregated where knowledgeable and sympathetic educators believe and can show that such separation is in the best interest of the child. However, it is recognized that the parents or guardians of these children have a right to participate in the decision-making process in such matters.

Cases concerning various disabilities have reached the conclusion that children and parents have the right to due process and equal protection *before* a child is identified as "exceptional" and *in the process* of determining her educational placement and also have the right to have the findings and placement periodically re-evaluated. Some of these cases related to children with such physical handicaps as loss of vision or hearing, others to youngsters who were mentally retarded or emotionally disturbed, or who had significant behavioral problems, specific learning disabilities or language handicaps. Examples could be given of thousands of children who were misdiagnosed as mentally retarded simply because their language was different from the one used to test them. Important steps have been taken to prevent such educational atrocities in the future.

Some states have taken such steps by passing laws specifically designed to protect the rights of "exceptional" children and their parents.* The most powerful law, however, is Public Law 94-142, a federal law generally known as the Education for All Handicapped Children Act of 1975.**

Since education is basically a function of state governments, this law provides for the education of handicapped children only indirectly: by making money available to states that comply with its provisions, which money is then turned over to Local Education Agencies (LEAs) if they

---

* Massachusetts, Wisconsin and Pennsylvania were the first states to enact such laws.

** Enacted on November 29, 1975.

meet the provisions of the law. Although indirect, this is an important way of upgrading the quality of education of "exceptional" children.

Public Law 94-142

In a preamble to the law, Congress states both its purpose and the facts on which it is based. The purposes are broad and bold: to assure that all handicapped children have available to them "a free appropriate public education and related services designed to meet their unique needs."

Among the facts the law discusses is the number of handicapped children in the United States today—over 8,000,000—and the inadequacy of provisions for their educational needs. More than a million of these children have been completely excluded from public schools, and many of those in school received inadequate education due to lack of supporting services or untrained teachers. Many parents were obliged to find tutors for their handicapped children or send them to private schools, often at great distance from home and at the parents' expense. Congress also found that, given adequate funding, we now know how to train teachers to provide effective special education for all children.

Key Provisions of P.L. 94-142

What age children will be educated under this law?

A "free appropriate public education" must be available to all handicapped children between the ages of 3 and 18 by September 1, 1978, and all children between the ages of 3 and 21 by September 1, 1980. Since education is primarily a state responsibility, P.L. 94-142 applies only to the age groups covered by the laws of the individual states. For example, if a state provides public schools from age 4 to 19, the federal law cannot extend that range from 3 to 21. Within each state the priority of funding must be as follows: 1) handicapped children currently not receiving an education, and 2) children with the most severe handicaps currently receiving inadequate education.

Where will handicapped children be educated?

They must be educated in the "least restrictive" educational environment appropriate to their needs. In other words, as much as possible and educationally appropriate, they should be educated with children who are not handicapped. This is what is meant by "mainstreaming." Among possible programs and plans, a regular public school class with appropriate support services is preferable to special classes; special classes are preferable to special schools; special schools might be preferable to home teaching; and home teaching is preferable to no teaching at all.

Furthermore, private schools are proper alternatives if no appropriate public facilities are available, and public funds should be used to support the education of the handicapped child in the private school. That school, of course, must meet the standards applied to state and local public schools.

What procedural safeguards protect parents and children under this law?

Policies and procedures designed to safeguard the rights of parents and children must include at least the following:

a. Access to all relevant school records;

b. Prior notice to parents of any proposed change in their child's educational placement or program and a written explanation of the procedures to be followed in effecting that change;

c. All communications with parents must be in the primary language of the parents; testing of children must not be discriminatory in language, race or culture;

d. Opportunity for a fair and impartial hearing to be conducted by the State Educational Agency (SEA) or local school district, *not* by the employee "involved in the education or care of the child." At any hearing, parents have the right to be represented by a lawyer or an individual trained in the problems of handicapped children; the right to present evidence; to subpoena, confront, and cross-examine witnesses; and to obtain a transcript of the hearing and a written decision by the hearing officer. Parents may appeal the decision to the SEA and, if they are still not satisfied, may appeal the SEA ruling in court;

e. The child has a right to remain in his or her current placement until the due process proceedings are completed. If the child is just beginning school, he or she may be enrolled in public school until then; and

f. A "surrogate parent" will be designated for children who are wards of the state or whose parents or guardians are unknown or unavailable.

Must there be individualized educational plans for each child?

Yes. The law provides that an individualized written plan must be developed for each handicapped child and reviewed annually by the child's parents and teachers, and a representative of the school district. The plan should indicate the child's present level of school performance, the educational services to be provided, and specific criteria to measure his progress.

School districts must maintain records of the individualized educational plans for each child.

Will there be adequately prepared educators to implement this law?

Recognizing the shortage of well prepared educators to meet the requirements of this new law, Congress included provisions for extensive personnel development. According to these provisions, Congress will supply funds to those states and local districts that develop plans for educating teachers and administrators in ways of dealing with the problems of handicapped students.

Will information about individual handicapped children be confidential?

Yes. The Secretary of the Department of Health, Education and Welfare must protect the confidentiality of personally identifiable information collected or maintained as a result of carrying out this law.

This landmark statute contains many other provisions, such as those related to formulas for allocating funds to states and to local school districts. But the major provisions of the law, those which directly affect the rights of parents and of children, are the ones presented above.

Summary

As difficult and expensive as it is to provide educational programs of sound quality for ordinary children, it is even more difficult and expensive to educate the handicapped. Until recently, and in many places even today, large numbers of handicapped children were segregated into special classes or special schools, or even excluded from public schooling. Parents who could afford it sent such children to private schools or hired tutors for them, but the vast majority received no formal education at all. Many of them became wards of the state, to be cared for in institutions, or became burdens on relatives.

Slowly a new view began to gain support that is making a dramatic change possible. Some of this change was brought about when parents and parent organizations went to court and demanded due process and equal protection for their children. Courts held that if a state provides public education for all of its children, it must do so without discriminating against the handicapped. They must be treated equitably and with respect for their procedural rights. In part that means that before any child can be excluded from school or placed under any label that brands him as inferior, adequate notice and a fair hearing must be provided. This concept has been accepted and enforced by courts in various states, has been enacted into law by several states, and was given powerful impetus when Congress passed the Education for All Handicapped Children Act of 1975.

According to the terms of this law, the federal government will make significant funds available to states to be used for special education. The states in turn will channel these funds to local schools. But the states and local schools must satisfy the federal guidelines. Thus local control and responsibility will be retained, yet federal standards and aid will help provide more appropriate schooling for handicapped children.

The law lists the rights that parents have to participate in the diagnosis, placement, education, and periodic re-evaluation of their children, and lists similar rights for the children. It points the way to a comprehensive approach to provide individualized educational programs, at public expense, for all handicapped children, in the least restrictive educational environment. It has been hailed by parents and educators alike as a major new development, perhaps one that can become a model for the education of all children.

It is anticipated that all states will be re-examining and revising their laws related to the education of the handicapped in order to comply with the federal law and thus qualify for substantial federal aid.

Chapter 13
Other Rights and Other Issues

This chapter discusses a number of issues that concern parents, not all of which are related to one another. Among them are: a statute that provides important rights for parents whose children do not speak English and a statute that provides important rights for poor parents and their children.* The chapter also examines such other topics as the financing of public education; the meaning of a "free" education; the openness of school board meetings; communications between student and school counselors; the use of schools by parent groups; and tracking and testing.

Title I, Parent Involvement

Title I of the Elementary and Secondary Education Act provides money for state and local education agencies to meet the educational needs of poor children. In 1976, almost two billion dollars were appropriated for this purpose. Moreover, no local school district can receive an allocation from these funds unless the parents of the children to be served are substantially involved.[4] To insure such involvement, local school districts are required in their application for funds to describe how parents of the children to be served (*1*) were consulted and involved in advance in planning the project and (*2*) the ways in which they will continue to be involved in its development and operation.

Parent Advisory Councils. School districts seeking funds under Title I are required to establish councils in which parents of educationally deprived children constitute at least a majority. Members of the councils are to be

---

* Two other statutes should be mentioned in passing, the Vocational Education Act, which provides that parents shall be members of the National Advisory Council,[1] and Title III of the Elementary and Secondary Education Act (ESEA) of 1965 which requires that parents be consulted with regard to the development of counselling services established at supplementary educational centers.[2]

given copies of the act and its regulations and other information needed for "the effective involvement, operation, and evaluation" of Title I projects. Parent councils must be given an adequate opportunity to review evaluations of prior Title I programs and to make recommendations concerning the educational needs that future programs should address and the services that should be provided to their children. In addition, school districts are required to establish procedures "to insure prompt response to complaints and suggestions from parents and parent councils." Moreover, schools are encouraged to develop for each child in a Title I project an "individualized, written educational plan," which must be agreed to by the child's parent. Some people believe that these procedures should be applied in *all* public schools, not merely those receiving Title I funds.

Non-English speaking parents and students

What are the rights of parents who speak little or no English?

Since their children must attend school, how can they learn if the language of instruction is English while the language spoken at home is not?

Until recently, children who spoke a language other than English had to sink or swim in school programs, since most states had laws requiring that English be the language of instruction. In recent years, several language minorities have challenged these laws as establishing an unfair requirement, and court fights as well as legislative efforts have been mounted for bilingual education. A major step in this direction was taken with the passage of the Bilingual Education Act of 1974.[5]

This statute was designed to meet the "special educational needs of large numbers of children of limited English speaking ability in the United States." It provides federal funds to states and local educational agencies for planning and developing bilingual programs and bilingual teacher education, as well as for early childhood and adult education, programs for dropouts, vocational programs, and courses in the history and culture of the language minority being served.

The law also provides funds for supplemental community activities, for fellowships and for program planning. It provides for classes in the students' own language and for classes in English-as-a-second-language but it stipulates that the children served by these classes shall attend the regular classes in such courses as music, art, and physical education, where language skill is not a major requirement for success. The law also gives parents important responsibility in planning programs, and requires that the students concerned be included in program planning and development in secondary schools.

Another act, the Equal Educational Opportunity Act of 1974,[6] also includes a useful section for those interested in furthering bilingual education. One of its sections states that an education agency which fails "to take appropriate action to overcome language barriers that impede equal participation by its students in its instructional programs" is in violation of the act.

It was under this provision that one of the best known cases in bilingual education was brought to court. The *Lau* case,[7] in San Francisco, California, was brought on behalf of Chinese speaking students who were at a disadvantage in classes where English was the language of instruction. Ruling in favor of the parents and children, the Supreme Court placed an affirmative obligation on schools to provide a meaningful educational program for non-English speaking students. Clearly, if students can't speak, read or write English, they are effectively excluded from an educational process conducted in English.

In addition to federal statutes and court cases, several states also have laws providing for bilingual education in their public schools. Among them are Massachusetts, Texas, Illinois and California.

Financing our Schools

Why do some schools have more money than others?

Most of the money that supports the public schools comes from local real-estate taxes. Some school districts have substantial income because the taxes that support them come from industries, businesses and expensive private homes. On the other hand, other school districts have to rely primarily on the taxes levied against poor or working-class homes. The result is that there are enormous differences in the financing of schools.

Do such large inequalities violate the Equal Protection Clause of the Constitution?

Some parents in Texas raised this question, on which the Supreme Court ruled in 1973 in the *Rodriguez* case.[8] The facts showed that Texas, like virtually every other state, contained both rich schools and poor schools and that the wealthy schools spent more money per pupil even though the property taxes were less burdensome than those paid in poor districts. The Court decided, nevertheless, that the Texas system of school finance did not violate the Constitution.

The U.S. Constitution contains no references to education, the Court pointed out. It is, therefore, not a fundamental federal right, and the remedy for inequitable school financing must be sought under state constitutions and laws. In its ruling the Court did not minimize the importance of education; but it placed responsibility for its financing on the states, noting that "the need is apparent for reform in tax systems which may well have relied too long and too heavily on the local property tax."

Developments Under State Laws

If parents cannot achieve equal funding for schools under the national Constitution, can they do so under state constitutions and statutes?

That depends on the laws of their respective states. While all our states are responsible for their public schools, all but Hawaii have delegated authority to local districts for school financing and management, and although these districts must meet the requirements of state laws, they nevertheless have substantial control over the schools. A number of states, recognizing the great disparities in school district wealth, have developed some type of equalization formula. But most of these attempts have not yet succeeded in equalizing school expenditures. Since most citizens value local control, they are reluctant to vote for statewide legislation which tells school districts just how much they may spend for education.

In addition to state legislative efforts, suits have been brought under state constitutions to achieve equalization. In New Jersey,[9] California,[10] and Connecticut,[11] such suits have been successful. In Arizona,[12] Washington,[13] and Idaho,[14] however, the courts have ruled against equalization efforts. There are two reasons for this disagreement among the courts: first, the specific wording in state constitutions differs; and second, constitutional provisions are often vague and abstract, making it possible for different judges to come up with different interpretations.

What is the way to equity in school finance? After dozens of lawsuits, many experts urge that solutions should be sought through legislation rather then judicial action. Furthermore, an increasing number of people questions whether complete equality in school financing is a desirable social policy. If we are to maintain local control of our schools, we may need to preserve the right of local districts to spend more money than the average on each child if they so choose. Through carefully drafted and properly administered laws, large discrepancies can be eliminated and substantial fairness accomplished in school financing. On the other hand, state imposed uniformity in school finance may insure equality at the cost of destroying educational freedom.* Some commentators believe that "equality at the cost of liberty can lead only to intellectual bankruptcy."[15] In all probability, efforts to achieve a proper balance between equality and liberty will continue in the courts and legislatures for some time.

Are public schools completely free?

Yes and no. Public schools are free in the sense that no fees can be charged for admission, attendance and basic instruction. However, there are disagreements among the 50 states concerning the provision of texts, instructional supplies, athletic equipment and uniforms, transportation of pupils, cost of transcripts and other incidental fees.

Each state's constitution and statutes must be interpreted to determine what is and is not included in free schooling in that state. A recent case in Colorado, for example, held that its state constitution does not mandate the provision of free books in the public schools for children of non-indigent parents.[16] ** Since a Colorado statute exists which requires school boards to provide books for children of indigent parents, the court concluded that the schools are *not* required to furnish free books for *all* pupils.

Most state constitutions provide for a "uniform system of free public education," a "system of free and common schools" or some similarly expressed system of public education. The Colorado case is but one example of disagreements over the interpretation of such provisions. For example, a New Mexico court ruled in 1976 that "a uniform system of free public

---

* A state could decide, for example, that it will allocate $900 per year per child in its schools. This would provide for equality in school finance. But what if the parents in school district A wanted to pay extra taxes to provide special teachers in art and instrumental music and thus spend $1000 per year per child? If parents are prevented from doing so, their liberty is curtailed; if they are allowed to proceed, equality suffers.

** Similar results were reached by courts in Arizona, Illinois, Indiana and Wisconsin, while courts ruled the other way in Idaho, Michigan and Montana.

schools" means that only required courses must be free, and that a fee may be charged for the others.[17] Some courts have upheld the power of schools to charge a reasonable fee for participation in extra-curricular activities, but have exempted from that fee students who do not participate.[18] *

Some school districts charge for pupil transportation, for field trips, and lab fees in chemistry classes. Parents must check the laws of their state to determine the legality of such charges in our "free" system of schooling.

Other Issues

May parents attend school board meetings?

In general, yes. All fifty states have statutes providing that meetings by such public bodies as school committees must be open. These "open meetings" laws also specify what matters may be conducted in executive sessions, which are closed to the public. Examples of items that may be discussed in executive sessions include sensitive personnel matters, law enforcement criminal information, employee disciplinary cases, collective bargaining strategy, gifts or bequests, and acquisition of real property. The law of each state specifies the items that may be discussed behind closed doors; all other matters should be considered in open meetings, called after proper public notice.[19]

Can parents find out what transpired between a school counselor and their children?

It depends on the state. For many years the law has protected the confidentiality of relationships between lawyers and clients, physicians and patients, priests and parishioners and psychiatrists and patients. But in the past, the courts did not extend this same privilege to school guidance counselors and their students. However, the situation is changing. Today, 13 states have laws which protect the confidentiality of the student-counselor relationship.** Parents must inquire concerning the laws of their own states in order to find out whether they have access to such information.

---

* A student had a right to one free transcript, though the school could charge a reasonable fee for subsequent ones.

** These states include: Connecticut, Idaho, Maine, Michigan, Montana, Nevada, North Carolina, North Dakota, Oregon, Pennsylvania, South Dakota, Washington, and the District of Columbia. *Students, Parents, and School Records,* William Rioux and Stuart Sandow, National Committee for Citizens in Education, Columbia, Maryland, (1974) p.5.

Tracking, Testing and Classification

Do parents have the right to object to track systems* in the schools?

Yes, they do, ruled a federal court in Washington, D.C.,[20] if it is shown that the tracking is based on socio-economic or racial discrimination. In the Washington case, students were placed in a track at the beginning of their school careers, and remained more or less locked into it for the rest of their schooling. Children who came from poor homes and from black families tended to be placed in the lower tracks and to remain there. Since Washington had a history of segregated and discriminatory schooling, the track system perpetuated separate and unequal education. The court therefore declared it a violation of the equal protection and due process clauses of the Constitution.

Does that mean that tracking is always unconstitutional?

No, it does not. If schools are very careful in forming tracks, if they keep them open and flexible so that students are not rigidly locked into one particular track early in their schooling, and if tracking is not based on racial, ethnic, socio-economic or other illegitimate criteria, the courts will not object to them.

May parents object to psychological testing in the schools?

The answer depends on the kind of testing, its purposes, and the way the test results are used. If, for example, the use of I.Q. tests places a disproportionate number of minority children in classes for the retarded, the burden is on the school district to show that the tests are valid, and there is a rational relationship between the way students are classified and a valid educational purpose.[21] If, on the other hand, the tests are fairly administered, if they are not culturally biased, and if they are administered in the students' own language, courts will uphold the schools' right to use them.[22]

May parent groups use school facilities for meetings?

In general, yes. State laws tend to give school boards authority to decide whether to make school buildings available to outside organizations for

---

* Tracking refers to a school organization that provides separate classes and curricula for students of different ability. For example, the four track systems in the *Hobson* case provided an honors curriculum for top ability students and then a regular, general, and basic curriculum for each of 3 groups of diminishing academic ability.

meetings or other activities. School boards generally extend such privileges upon compliance with certain reasonable rules. But on occasion, a request for the use of school facilities may be refused. In 1976, an Oklahoma school board denied a PTA the use of a school building for its meeting, because its rules specified that it would "not tolerate unsupportive organizations" or those that "deal in personalities or engage in frequent criticism against the school system and the school personnel in particular . . . ." [23]

When the PTA brought the school board to court, the Oklahoma Supreme Court ruled in favor of the PTA on the grounds that the board's rules violated the freedom of speech provision of the First Amendment, the equal protection clause of the Fourteenth Amendment and similar provisions of the Oklahoma constitution. A school board may close its facilities to all outside groups, the court said, or it may establish reasonable standards to determine availability. But it may not violate the provisions of the Constitution or state law. If a school district allows the use of facilities to some outside organizations, it must not unreasonably discriminate against others.

Summary

Title I of the Elementary and Secondary Education Act grants money to every state to meet the needs of educationally deprived children. Its regulations require substantial involvement of the parents of the children served in the planning, development, implementation and evaluation of all Title I projects. The Bilingual Education Act is another federal law that provides additional rights for parents. It attempts to meet the special needs of children with limited ability to speak English and provides a variety of educational programs designed to involve them and their parents.

Although the Supreme Court has ruled that the unequal financing of public schools does not violate the U.S. Constitution, parents may still challenge this practice in state legislatures or local courts. Some state courts have held unequal financing illegal while others have not found this practice unconstitutional.

State provisions for "free" public education have generally meant that no fees can be charged for admission, attendance, and required courses. But states differ concerning whether public schools can charge for books, elective courses, laboratory fees, and extra-curricular activities.

Statutes in every state provide that meetings of public bodies such as school committees be open; but many of these laws also specify that certain sensitive matters may be discussed in closed sessions. The common law generally does not protect the confidentiality of discussions between students and school counselors; but 13 states have passed statutes which specifically protect this relationship. Parents may object to tracking, or other classifications of their children based on racial or socio-economic discrimination. However, when such classifications are based on legitimate educational criteria, they are permissible.

A school board has no legal obligation to make its facilities available to any outside group. But if it does allow some organizations to use its buildings, it must make them equally available to all and cannot prohibit their use by a group because it considers the group's actions unsupportive of the public schools.

Chapter 14
Toward Legal Literacy for All

During their schooling, most parents learned nothing about the law, except, perhaps, a few historic cases. Today, many schools still teach little about our legal system that is relevant and useful, concentrating instead on presenting an idealized version of our system of government or preaching the importance of respecting and obeying the law while simultaneously violating the rights of parents and students. Instead of increasing respect for law, this approach often promotes cynicism toward it.

In recent years, however, a new approach has been developed by lawyers and educators which gives students a more realistic understanding of the legal system and its relevance to their lives. By learning how the system can work for them, they gain a greater understanding and appreciation of our laws and develop a personal investment in supporting and improving our legal system.

This personal and dynamic approach to law-related education (or law studies) is becoming an increasingly important part of education throughout the country. Part of its success is due to the innovative methods and excellent materials that have been developed for teaching about law in the public schools. The American Bar Association Committee on Youth Education for Citizenship has published a series of useful booklets that can help parents become better informed about these programs, including an annotated bibliography of printed and audiovisual curriculum materials as well as a list of educational projects in each state.

Most law materials are incorporated into social studies courses, and many are offered as high school electives. They include materials ranging from a theoretical and philosophical approach to courses focusing on constitutional law to practical questions of criminal, contract, consumer, and environmental law. In addition, law studies include a variety of popular teaching techniques such as mock trials, role playing, and case analysis. Many courses bring lawyers or law enforcement personnel into the classroom or visit courts, prisons, and police stations. (More about these booklets and materials and where they can be obtained is included at the end of this chapter.)

Most schools that have introduced law into the curriculum have found that the experience is popular with teachers and parents as well as students —in elementary as well as secondary grades. Even so, less than 20% of our students have been exposed to law-related education. Parents can help expand these programs and promote universal legal literacy in several ways:

1. By encouraging schools to begin programs in law-related education. (Some parents learn as much from these programs as their children.)

2. By encouraging teachers and administrators to extend these programs to the "hidden curriculum" in schools where it is already part of the formal curriculum. This "hidden curriculum" is contained in the way schools teach through their policies and practices, rather than their texts and lessons. For example, schools teach as much (or more) about due process by the way they develop and implement their disciplinary codes as by what teachers say about this constitutional concept in class. Therefore, it is crucial to help schools realize the importance of having their hidden curriculum complement and reinforce their official curriculum.

3. By encouraging and assisting your children's schools to begin (or extend) their efforts to keep all students, parents, and teachers informed about their rights and responsibilities under federal, state, and local laws and regulations. As education law changes and expands, this needs to be done on a continuing basis—with regular written communications and annual or semi-annual meetings or workshops.

Teachers, for example, can be taught about education law in courses or workshops sponsored by school districts, teacher organizations, or state colleges. And parents can be educated about their rights and responsibilities at PTA meetings, school-sponsored workshops, community college courses, or through parent newsletters and magazines. In addition to discussing the kinds of information included in this book, such meetings or workshops could examine the ways in which federal laws and judicial decisions affecting parents' rights are carried out in your state and community. Local school administrators could be invited to discuss specific ways parents can participate in formulating policy and suggesting changes concerning school rules, texts, curriculum or personnel matters. Representatives from your state department of education could be invited to explain new state policies or programs and how they affect your schools and children. Or an attorney who is familiar with education law might discuss recent judicial decisions of interest to parents in your community.

If parents, teachers and students are legally literate, each group's rights will be strengthened. In some legal areas, promoting the rights of one group may curtail the rights of another. But this is generally not the case with respect to parents' rights. For example, if schools do not respect the freedom of expression or due process rights of teachers, this will not expand the rights of parents. On the contrary; it will make it more likely that parental rights will also be ignored. Conversely, school districts that respect the free speech or due process rights of teachers and students are more likely to be aware and respectful of these parental rights as well.

Agenda for the Future. As we find ourselves in a judicial era dominated by a conservative Supreme Court, some people are concerned that the courts will not continue to expand the rights of students and parents in the future as they have in the past. While this is probably true, we do not find the prospect threatening, because we do not believe that the judicial expansion of parent and student rights is the major issue today. It is far more important to help parents and educators become aware both of the legal rights that parents and students already have and of ways of protecting these rights in the public schools. The courts are not the only place that parents can turn to, to protect and expand their rights. There are parent councils, school administrators, and local school boards; state legislatures and state departments and boards of education; the federal Office of Education, Congress, and national citizen and parent organizations. Each of these groups can influence what happens in your school and most provide ways for interested parents to learn more about their rights and to influence public education.

Helping all citizens of the school community learn about their rights and responsibilities will create a climate in which each individual will be more appreciative of the law and respectful of the rights of others. By teaching law through the formal and hidden curriculum to parents and teachers as well as students, our public schools can reaffirm their historic role of educating all Americans for more effective citizenship in a democratic society.

NOTES

Chapter 1

[1] *Pierce* v. *Society of Sisters*, 268 U.S. 510 (1924).

[2] *Wisconsin* v. *Yoder,* 406 U.S. 205 (1972).

[3] *Goss* v. *Lopez*, 419 U.S. 565 (1975).

[4] *Tinker* v. *Des Moines*, 393 U.S. 503 (1969).

[5] *Wood* v. *Strickland,* 420 U.S. 308 (1975)

[6] *A Study of State Legal Standards for the Provision of Public Education,* Lawyers Committee for Civil Rights Under Law, National Institute of Education, Washington, D.C. (1974).

Chapter 2

[1] *Goss* v. *Lopez*, 419 U.S. 565 (1975).

[2] Robert L. Ackerly, *The Reasonable Exercise of Authority*, Washington, D.C. National Association of Secondary School Principals, 1969, pp. 14-16.

[3] *Baker* v. *Owens*, 423 U.S. 907 (1975).

[4] *Ingraham* v. *Wright*, 97 S. Ct. 1401 (1977).

[5] *People* v. *Overton,* 249 N.E.2d 366 (N.Y. 1969)

[6] *Matter of Carroll,* Decision of Chancellor (N.Y., Dec. 6, 1971).

Chapter 3

[1] *Tinker* v. *Des Moines Independent School District*, 393 U.S. 503 (1969)

[2] *Guzick* v. *Debras*, 431 F.2d 594 (6th Cir. 1970), *cert. denied*, 401 U.S. 948 (1971).

[3] *Shanley* v. *Northeast Independent School District*, 462 F.2d 960 (5th Cir. 1972).

[4] *Ibid.*

[5] *Fujishima* v. *Board of Education*, 460 F.2d 1355 (7th Cir. 1972); *Riseman* v. *School Committee of Quincy*, 439 F.2d 148 (1st Cir. 1971).

[6] *Shanley* v. *Northeast Independent School District*, 462 F.2d 960 (5th Cir. 1972); *Eisner* v. *Stamford Board of Education*, 440 F.2d 803 (2nd Cir. 1971).

[7] *Miller* v. *California*, 413 U.S. 13 (1973).

[8] *Zucker* v. *Panitz*, 299 F. Supp. 102 (S.D. N.Y. 1968).

[9] *Dickey* v. *Alabama State Board of Education*, 273 F.Supp. 613 (M.D. Ala. 1967).

[10] *Vail* v. *Board of Education of Portsmouth*, 354 F.Supp. 592 (D. N.H. 1973).

Chapter 4

[1] *Pierce* v. *Society of Sisters*, 268 U.S. 510 (1925).

[2] *Wisconsin* v. *Yoder*, 406 U.S. 205 (1972).

[3] *Barnette* v. *West Virginia*, 319 U.S. 624 (1943).

[4] *Banks* v. *Board of Public Instruction of Dade County*, 314 F.Supp. 285 (S.D. Fla. 1970).

[5] *Abington School District* v. *Schempp*, 374 U.S. 203 (1963) and *Engel* v. *Vitale*, 370 U.S. 421 (1962).

[6] *Gaines* v. *Anderson*, 421 F.Supp. 337 (D. Mass. 1976).

[7] *Spence* v. *Bailey*, 465 F.2d 797 (6th Cir. 1972).

[8] *Hardwick* v. *Board of School Trustees*, 205 P. 49 (Cal. 1921).

[9] *F. and F.* v. *Duval County*, 273 So.2d 15 (Fla. 1973).

[10] *Zorach* v. *Clausen*, 343 U.S. 306 (1952).

[11] *Everson* v. *Board of Education*, 330 U.S. 1 (1947).

[12] *Board of Education* v. *Allen*, 392 U.S. 236 (1968).

[13] See for example *Meek* v. *Pittinger*, 421 U.S. 349 (1975).

[14] *Wolman* v. *Walter*, 97 S.Ct. 2593 (1977).

Chapter 5

[1] *Arnold* v. *Carpenter*, 459 F.2d 939 (7th Cir. 1972).

[2] *Richards* v. *Thurston*, 424 F.2d 1281 (1st Cir. 1970).

[3] *Bishop* v. *Colaw*, 450 F.2d 1069 (8th Cir. 1971).

[4] *Massie* v. *Henry*, 455 F.2d 779 (4th Cir. 1972).

[5] *Zeller* v. *Donegal School District Board of Education*, 517 F.2d 600 (3rd Cir. 1975).

[6] *King* v. *Saddleback*, 445 F.2d 932 (9th Cir. 1971).

[7] *Freeman* v. *Flake*, 448 F.2d 258 (10th Cir. 1971).

[8] *Jackson* v. *Dorrier*, 424 F.2d 213 (6th Cir. 1970).

[9] *Karr* v. *Schmidt*, 460 F.2d 609 (5th Cir. 1972).

[10] *Karr* v. *Schmidt*, 401 U.S. 1202 (1971).

[11] *Dwen* v. *Barry*, 483 F.2d 1126 (2d Cir. 1973).

[12] *Kelley* v. *Johnson*, 425 U.S. 238 (1976).

[13] *Syrek* v. *Pennsylvania*, 537 F.2d 66 (3rd Cir. 1976).

[14] *Zeller* v. *Donegal*, 517 F.2d 600 (3rd Cir. 1975).

[15] *Fagan* v. *National Cash Register Co.*, 481 F.2d 1115 (D.C. Cir. 1973).

[16] *Bannister* v. *Paradis*, 316 F.Supp. 185 (D. N.H. 1970).

[17] *Scott* v. *Board of Education, Hicksville*, 305 N.Y.S.2d 601 (1969)

[18] *Wallace* v. *Ford*, 346 F.Supp. 156 (E.D. Ark. 1972).

[19] *Dunham* v. *Pulsifer*, 312 F.Supp. 411, 419 (D. Vt. 1970).

(Continued on next page)

Chapter 5—*(Continued)*

[20] *Arnold* v. *Carpenter*, 459 F.2d 939, 944 (7th Cir. 1972).
[21] *Buckholz* v. *Leveille*, 194 N.W.2d 427 (Mich. 1972).
[22] *Bannister* v. *Paradis*, 316 F.Supp. 185 (D. N.H. 1970).

Chapter 6

[1] *Brown* v. *Board of Education*, 347 U.S. 483 (1954).
[2] Id. at 495.
[3] *Brown* v. *Board of Education*, 349 U.S. 294 (1955).
[4] *Swann* v. *Charlotte-Mecklenburg Board of Education*, 402 U.S. 1 (1971).
[5] Id. at 9-10.
[6] Id. at 29.
[7] *Milliken* v. *Bradley*, 418 U.S. 717 (1974).
[8] Ibid.
[9] *Green* v. *County School Board of New Kent Co., Va.*, 391 U.S. 430 (1968).
[10] *Morgan* v. *Kerrigan*, 409 F.Supp. 1141 (D. Mass. 1975).
[11] *Pasadena City Board of Education* v. *Spangler*, 96 S.Ct. 416 (1976).

Chapter 7

[1] Title IX of the Education Amendments of 1972, 20 U.S.C. 1681.
[2] *Brenden* v. *Independent School District 742*, 477 F.2d 1292 (8th Cir. 1973).
[3] Id. at 1233.
[4] See, for example, Ch. 622 of the Massachusetts General Laws.
[5] *Vorchheimer* v. *School District of Philadelphia*, 532 F.2d 880 (3rd Cir. 1976). (Affirmed in a 4-4 decision by the Supreme Court. Such a split decision has no value as precedent.)
[6] *Bray* v. *Lee*, 377 F.Supp. 934 (D. Mass. 1972).
[7] *Berkelman* v. *San Francisco Unified School District*, 501 F.2d 1264 (9th Cir. 1974).
[8] See Brian E. Berwick and Carol Oppenheimer, "Marriage, Pregnancy, and the Right to Go to School," 50 *Texas Law Review*, 1196-1228 (1972).
[9] *Kissick* v. *Garland Independent School District*, 330 S.W.2d 708 (Tex. 1959).
[10] *Bell* v. *Lone Oak Indep. School District*, 507 S.W.2d 636 (Tex. 1974).
[11] *Davis* v. *Meek*, 344 F.Supp. 298 (N.D. Ohio 1972).

Chapter 8

[1] *Sheehan* v. *St. Peter's Catholic School,* 188 N.W.2d 868 (Minn. 1971).
[2] *Mancha* v. *Field Museum of Natural History,* 283 N.E.2d 899 (Ill. 1972).
[3] *LaValley* v. *Stanford,* 70 N.Y.S.2d 460 (1947).
[4] *Damguard* v. *Oakland High School District,* 298 Pac. 983 (Cal. 1931).
[5] *Severson* v. *City of Beloit,* 167 N.W.2d 258 (Wisc. 1969).
[6] *Nash* v. *Rapides Parish School Board,* 188 So.2d 508 (La. 1966).
[7] *Kaufman* v. *City of New York,* 214 N.Y.S.2d 767 (1969).
[8] *Gilcrease* v. *Speight,* 6 So.2d 95 (La. 1942).
[9] *Frace* v. *Long Beach City High School District,* 137 P.2d 60 (Cal. 1943).
[10] 57 Am. Jur.2d *Negligence* § 363 (1971).
[11] 57 Am. Jur.2d *Negligence* § 431 (1976 Supplement).
[12] Id., § 426.
[13] *Vendrell* v. *School District No. 26C,* 360 P.2d 282 (Ore. 1961).
[14] *Mogabgab* v. *Orleans Parish School District,* 239 S.2d 456 (La. 1970).
[15] *Ayala* v. *Philadelphia Board of Public Education,* 305 A.2d 877, 881 (Pa. 1973).
[16] Id. at 889; and see note 8, *Davies* v. *City of Bath,* 364 A.2d 1269, 1272 (Me. 1976).
[17] 66 Am. Jur.2d *Release* § 14, 33 (1971).
[18] *Elder* v. *Anderson,* 23 Cal.Rptr. 48 (1962).
[19] *Martin* v. *Kearney,* 124 Cal.Rptr. 281 (1975).
[20] *Segall* v. *Piazza,* 260 N.Y.S.2d 543 (1965).
[21] *Wood* v. *Strickland,* 420 U.S. 308 (1975).

Chapter 9

[1] *Peter W. Doe* v. *San Francisco School District,* 131 Cal.Rptr. 854 (1976).
[2] New York Times, September 11, 1977.
[3] NOLPE Notes, National Organization on Legal Problems In Education, July, 1977, page 3.
[4] American Educator, Summer, 1977, page 6.
[5] "Update VI: Minimal Competency Testing," Chris Pipho, Education Commission of the States, Denver, Colorado, June 1, 1977.
[6] *Epperson* v. *Arkansas,* 393 U.S. 97 (1968).
[7] *Cornwell* v. *State Board of Education,* 314 F.Supp. 340 (D. Md. 1968), 428 F.2d 471 (4th Cir. 1970).
[8] *Citizens for Parental Rights* v. *San Mateo Co. Bd. of Ed.,* 124 Cal.Rptr. 68 (1975).

(Continued on next page)

Chapter 9—*(Continued)*

[9] *Williams* v. *Bd. of Education of Cty. of Kanawha,* 388 F.Supp. 93 (S.D. W.Va. 1975).

[10] *Keefe* v. *Geanakos,* 418 F.2d 359 (1st Cir. 1969).

[11] *Miller* v. *California,* 413 U.S. 15 (1973).

[12] *Grosser* v. *Woollett,* 341 N.E.2d 356 (Ohio 1974).

[13] *Rosenberg* v. *Board of Education of City of New York,* 92 N.Y.S.2d 344 (1949).

[14] *Minarcini* v. *Strongsville City School District,* 541 F.2d 577 (6th Cir. 1976).

[15] *Presidents Council, Dist. 25* v. *Community School Board No. 25,* 457 F.2d 289 (2nd Cir. 1972).

[16] *Mass. G.L. Ch. 71, §3, 1972.*

[17] "A Compendium of State Legal Standards for the Provision of Public Education 1974-75," Lawyers' Committee for Civil Rights Under Law, Washington, D.C., N.I.E. (D.H.E.W.), 1976.

Chapter 10

[1] *Pierce* v. *Society of Sisters,* 268 U.S. 510 (1924).

[2] *Scoma* v. *Chicago Board of Education,* 391 F.Supp. 452 (N.D. Ill. 1974).

[3] *Board of Education of Central School District No. 1* v. *Allen,* 392 U.S. 236 (1968).

[4] *State* v. *Whisner,* 351 N.E.2d 750 (Ohio 1976).

[5] *People* v. *Levisen,* 90 N.E.2d (Ill. 1950).

[6] *In Re Foster,* 330 N.Y.S.2d 8 (1972).

[7] *Knox* v. *O'Brien,* 72 A.2d 389 (N.J. 1950).

[8] *State* v. *Massa,* 231 A.2d 252 (N.J. 1967).

[9] *State* v. *Superior Court,* 346 P.2d 999 (Wash. 1960).

[10] *People* v. *Turner,* 263 P.2d 685 (Cal. 1953).

[11] *Matter of Franz,* 390 N.Y.S.2d 940 (1977).

[12] *State ex rel. Sheibley* v. *School District No. 1,* 48 N.W. 393 (Neb. 1891).

[13] *State ex rel. Kelley* v. *Ferguson,* 144 N.W. 1039 (Neb. 1914).

[14] *People ex rel. Vollmar* v. *Stanley,* 255 P. 610 (Colo. 1927).

[15] "Parental Rights and Responsibilities" Joel S. Moskowitz, 50 Washington Law Review 623 (1975).

[16] *Hardwick* v. *Board of School Trustees,* 205 P. 49 (Cal. 1921).

[17] *Valent* v. *New Jersey State Board of Education,* 274 A.2d 832 (N.J. 1971), reversed on procedural grounds 288 A.2d 52 (N.J. 1972).

[18] *Zebra* v. *School District of City of Pittsburgh,* 296 A.2d 748 (Pa. 1972).

(Continued on next page)

Chapter 10—*(Continued)*

[19] *Commonwealth ex rel. Sch. Dist. of Pittsburgh* v. *Ross,* 330 A.2d 290 (Pa. 1975).

[20] *In re Foster,* 330 N.Y.S.2d 8 (1972).

[21] "A Compedium of State Legal Standards for the Provision of Public Education 1974-75," Lawyers' Committee for Civil Rights under Law, Washington, D.C, N.I.E. (D.H.E.W.) 1976.

Chapter 11

[1] "Cumulative Records: Assault on Privacy," Diane Divoky, *Learning Magazine,* p. 9, September 1973.

[2] *Ibid.*

[3] "Off the Record: The Emerging Right to Control One's School Files," Michael Stone, 5 *N.Y.U. Review of Law and Social Change,* 39 (1975).

[4] *Id.,* at 42.

[5] *Van Allen* v. *McCleary,* 211 N.Y.S.2d 501 (1961).

[6] Stone, *Supra,* p. 48.

[7] Divorky, *Supra,* p. 10.

[8] The text of the Act is contained in 20 U.S.C. § 1232 g. Final Regulations to implement the Act were issued by the Department of Health, Education, and Welfare and were published in the Federal Register, June 17, 1976; 45 C.F.R. § 99 (1976).

Chapter 12

[1] *Pennsylvania Association for Retarded Children* v. *Commonwealth of Pennsylvania,* 343 F.Supp. 279 (E.D. Pa. 1972).

[2] *Mills* v. *Board of Education of the District of Columbia,* 348 F.Supp. 866 (D. D.C. 1972).

Chapter 13

[1] P.L. 94-482 Title I, Vocational Education Act, 162 (a) (12) 1976.

[2] 45 C.F.R. § 118.11 (b) (1976).

[3] *Digest of Educational Statistics 1975 Edition,* Grant and Lund, U.S. Gov't Printing Office, Washington, D.C., p. 159.

[4] 45 C.F.R. § 116 (1976). See especially § 116.17 (o) and 116 a. 25.

(Continued on next page)

Chapter 13—*(Continued)*

[5] 20 U.S.C.A. 880b. The 1974 statute builds on the Bilingual Act of 1968.

[6] 20 U.S.C. 1701.

[7] *Lau* v. *Nichols*, 414 U.S. 563 (1974).

[8] *San Antonio Independent School District* v. *Rodriguez*, 411 U.S. 1 (1973).

[9] *Robinson* v. *Cahill*, 303 A.2d 273 (N.J. 1973).

[10] *Serrano* v. *Priest*, 557 P.2d 929 (Cal. 1976).

[11] *Hopton* v. *Meskill*, 332 A.2d 113 (Conn. 1974).

[12] *Shofstall* v. *Hollins*, 515 P.2d 590 (Ariz. 1973).

[13] *Northshore School District No. 417* v. *Kinnear*, 530 P.2d 178 (Wash. 1974).

[14] *Thompson* v. *Engelking*, 537 P.2d 635 (Idaho 1975).

[15] Nathan S. Kline, M.D., Columbia U., Bergman lecture, Feb. 8, 1976, in Westhampton, New York.

[16] *Marshall* v. *School District Re #3 Morgan County, Colorado*, 553 P.2d 784 (Colo. 1976).

[17] *Norton* v. *Board of Education of School District No. 16*, 553 P.2d 1277 (N.M. 1976).

[18] *Paulson* v. *Minidoka County School District No. 331*, 463 P.2d 935 (Idaho 1970).

[19] "A Summary of Freedom of Information and Privacy Laws of the 50 States," Wallis E. McClain, Ed., Access Reports, 2626 Pennsylvania Ave., N.W., Washington, D.C. 20037.

[20] *Hobson* v. *Hansen*, 269 F.Supp. 401 (D.D.C. 1967).

[21] *Larry P.* v. *Riles*, 343 F.Supp. 1306 (N.D. Calif. 1972).

[22] *Murray et al* v. *West Baton Rouge Parish School Board et al.*, 472 F.2d 438 (5th Cir. 1973).

[23] *Hennesey* v. *Independent School District No. 4, Lincoln City*, 552 P.2d 1141 (Okl. 1976).

Appendix A
Constitutional Amendments
(Most Relevant to the Rights of Parents and Students)

AMENDMENT I

Congress shall make no law respecting an establishment of religion, or prohibiting the free exercise thereof; or abridging the freedom of speech, or of the press; or the right of the people peaceably to assemble, and to petition the Government for a redress of grievances.

AMENDMENT IV

The right of the people to be secure in their persons, houses, papers, and effects against unreasonable searches and seizures, shall not be violated, and no Warrants shall issue, but upon probable cause, supported by Oath or affirmation, and particularly describing the place to be searched, and the persons or things to be seized.

AMENDMENT V

No person shall be held to answer for a capital, or otherwise infamous crime, unless on a presentment or indictment of a Grand Jury, except in cases arising in the land or naval forces, or in the Militia, when in actual service in time of War or public danger; nor shall any person be subject for the same offense to be twice put in jeopardy of life or limb; nor shall be compelled in any criminal case to be a witness against himself, nor be deprived of life, liberty, or property, without due process of law; nor shall private property be taken for public use, without just compensation.

AMENDMENT IX

The enumeration in the Constitution, of certain rights, shall not be construed to deny or disparage others retained by the people.

AMENDMENT X

The powers not delegated to the United States by the Constitution, nor prohibited by it to the States, are reserved to the States respectively, or to the people.

AMENDMENT XIV

Section 1 All persons born or naturalized in the United States, and subject to the jurisdiction thereof, are citizens of the United States and of the State wherein they reside. No State shall make or enforce any law which shall abridge the privileges or immunities of citizens of the United States; nor shall any State deprive any person of life, liberty, or property, without due process of law; nor deny to any person within its jurisdiction the equal protection of the laws.

PROPOSED EQUAL RIGHTS AMENDMENT

Equality of rights under the law shall not be denied or abridged by the United States or by any state on account of sex.

Appendix B
How Can You Find Reports of Court Cases?

It is not too difficult to find a law library. Every law school has one; many universities have collections of law books, and lawyers, too have their law libraries. In each of these places a librarian or friend can help parents find cases of interest to them. The following is offered as a start into the mysteries of legal research, which is neither as mysterious or as complicated as many laymen believe.

Appellate courts generally publish their decisions. The highest of these, the Supreme Court, publishes its most recent decisions in a weekly loose leaf volume called *United States Law Week*. A citation in this volume looks like the following:

Richard M. Nixon v. *Administrator of General Services*
45 U.S.L.W. 4917 (June 28, 1977).

This citation gives us the names of the parties to the suit, with the party appealing to the Supreme Court listed first. The entry further indicates that the case is reported in volume 45 of *United States Law Week*, beginning at page 4917, and that the decision was rendered on June 28, 1977. Less recent Supreme Court cases can be found in the *United States Reports*. For example, the citation *Brown* v. *Board of Education of Topeka, Kansas*, 347 U.S. 483 (1954), refers to volume 347 of the *United States Reports* at page 483 and indicates that the decision was handed down in 1954.

Cases decided by the federal District Courts are reported in a publication entitled *Federal Supplement*, while those of the United States Courts of Appeals are reported in the *Federal Reporter, Second Series*. *Carmical* v. *Craven*, 547 F.2d 1380 (1977), would indicate that this case is reported in volume 547 of the *Federal Reporter, Second Series*, beginning at page 1380, decided in 1977. Similarly, *Cook* v. *Brockway*, 424 F.Supp. 1046

(1977), would be found in volume 434 of the *Federal Supplement* at page 1046.

Decisions of state appeals courts are reported in regional reporters. For example *Shrum* v. *Zeltwanger*, Wyo., 559 P.2d 1384 (1977), indicates that this is a Wyoming Case, reported in volume 559 of the *Pacific Reporter, Second Series*, at page 1384, while *Price* v. *School Board of Broward County*, Florida App. 342 So.2d 1039 (1977), is a Florida case reported in volume 342 of the *Southern Reporter, Second Series*, at page 1039.

The numbering system is consistent in official legal publications, while the titles of the reporters vary to reflect the courts, regions or states for which they report cases. The foregoing should enable the reader to find any case cited in this book. For other aids to legal research, including encyclopedias and digests, a friendly librarian is most helpful.

Appendix C
Excerpts from Supreme Court Decisions of Interest to Parents and Students

TINKER v. DES MOINES
Feb. 24, 1969

Mr. Justice Fortas delivered the opinion of the Court.

Petitioner John F. Tinker, 15 years old, and petitioner Christopher Eckhardt, 16 years old, attended high schools in Des Moines, Iowa. Petitioner Mary Beth Tinker, John's sister, was a 13-year-old student in junior high school.

In December 1965, a group of adults and students in Des Moines held a meeting at the Eckhardt home. The group determined to publicize their objections to the hostilities in Vietnam and their support for a truce by wearing black armbands during the holiday season and by fasting on December 16 and New Year's Eve. Petitioners and their parents had previously engaged in similar activities, and they decided to participate in the program.

The principals of the Des Moines schools became aware of the plan to wear armbands. On December 14, 1965, they met and adopted a policy that any student wearing an armband to school would be asked to remove it, and if he refused he would be suspended until he returned without the armband. Petitioners were aware of the regulation that the school authorities adopted.

On December 16, Mary Beth and Christopher wore black armbands to their schools. John Tinker wore his armband the next day. They were all sent home and suspended from school until they would come back without their armbands. They did not return to school until after the planned period for wearing armbands had expired—that is, until after New Year's Day.

I.

As we shall discuss, the wearing of armbands in the circumstances of this case was entirely divorced from actually or potentially disruptive conduct by those participating in it. It was closely akin to "pure speech" which, we have repeatedly held, is entitled to comprehensive protection under the First Amendment.

First Amendment rights, applied in light of the special characteristics of the school environment, are available to teachers and students. It can hardly be argued that either students or teachers shed their constitutional rights to freedom of speech or expression at the schoolhouse gate. This has been the unmistakable holding of this Court for almost 50 years.

In West Virginia State Board of Education v. Barnette, the Court said:

> "The Fourteenth Amendment, as now applied to the States, protects the citizen against the State itself and all of its creatures—Boards of Education not excepted. These have, of course, important, delicate, and highly discretionary functions, but none that they may not perform within the limits of the Bill of Rights. That they are educating the young for citizenship is reason for scrupulous protection of Constitutional freedoms of the individual, if we are not to strangle the free mind at its source and teach youth to discount important principles of our government as mere platitudes."

On the other hand, the Court has repeatedly emphasized the need for affirming the comprehensive authority of the States and of school officials, consistent with fundamental constitutional safeguards, to prescribe and control conduct in the schools. Our problem lies in the area where students in the exercise of First Amendment rights collide with the rules of the school authorities.

II.

Only a few of the 18,000 students in the school system wore the black armbands. Only five students were suspended for wearing them. There is no indication that the work of the schools or any class was disrupted. Outside the classrooms, a few students made hostile remarks to the children wearing armbands, but there were no threats or acts of violence on school premises.

The District Court concluded that the action of the school authorities was reasonable because it was based upon their fear of a disturbance from the wearing of the armbands. But, in our system, undifferentiated fear or apprehension of disturbance is not enough to overcome the right to freedom of expression. Any departure from absolute regimentation may cause trouble. Any variation from the majority's opinion may inspire fear. Any word spoken, in class, in the lunchroom, or on the campus, that deviates from the views of another person may start an argument or cause a disturbance. But our Constitution says we must take this risk, and our history says that it is this sort of hazardous freedom—this kind of openness—that is the basis of our national strength and of the independence and vigor of Americans who grow up and live in this relatively permissive, often disputatious, society.

In order for the State in the person of school officials to justify prohibition of a particular expression of opinion, it must be able to show that its action was caused by something more than a mere desire to avoid the discomfort and unpleasantness that always accompany an unpopular viewpoint. Certainly where there is no finding and no showing that engaging in the forbidden conduct would "materially and substantially interfere with the requirements of appropriate discipline in the operation of the school," the prohibition cannot be sustained.

In the present case, school authorities did not purport to prohibit the wearing of all symbols of political or controversial significance. The record shows that students in some of the schools wore buttons relating to national political campaigns, and some even wore the Iron Cross, traditionally a symbol of Nazism. The order prohibiting the wearing of armbands did not extend to these. Instead, a particular symbol—black armbands worn to exhibit opposition to this Nation's involvement in Vietnam—was singled out for prohibition. Clearly, the prohibition of expression of one particular opinion, at least without evidence that it is necessary to avoid material and substantial interference with schoolwork or discipline, is not constitutionally permissible.

In our system, state-operated schools may not be enclaves of totalitarianism. School officials do not possess absolute authority over their students. Students in school as well as out of school are "persons" under our Constitution. They are possessed of fundamental rights which the State must respect, just as they themselves must respect their obligations to the State. In our system, students may not be regarded as closed-circuit recipients of only that which the State chooses to communicate. They may not be confined to the expression of those sentiments that are officially approved. In the absence of a specific showing of constitutionally valid reasons to regulate their speech, students are entitled to freedom of expression of their views. As Judge Gewin, speaking for the Fifth Circuit, said, school officials cannot suppress "expressions of feelings with which they do not wish to contend."

In Meyer v. Nebraska, Mr. Justice McReynolds expressed this Nation's repudiation of the principle that a State might so conduct its schools as to "foster a homogeneous people." He said:

> "In order to submerge the individual and develop ideal citizens, Sparta assembled the males at seven into barracks and entrusted their subsequent education and training to official guardians. Although such measures have been deliberately approved by men of great genius, their ideas touching the relation between individual and State were wholly different from those upon which our institutions rest; and it hardly will be affirmed that any Legislature could impose such restrictions upon the people of a state without doing violence to both letter and spirit of the Constitution.

This principle has been repeated by this Court on numerous occasions during the intervening years. Mr. Justice Brennan, speaking for the Court, said:

> "The vigilant protection of constitutional freedoms is nowhere more vital than in the community of American schools. The classroom is peculiarly the 'marketplace of ideas.' The Nation's future depends upon leaders trained through wide exposure to that robust exchange of ideas which discovers truth 'out of a multitude of tongues,' [rather] than through any kind of authoritative selection."

The principle of these cases is not confined to the supervised and ordained discussion which takes place in the classroom. The principal use to which the schools are dedicated is to accommodate students during prescribed hours for the purpose of certain types of activities. Among those activities is personal intercommunication among the students. This is not only an inevitable part of the process of attending school; it is also an important part of the educational process. A student's rights, therefore, do not embrace merely the classroom hours. When he is in the cafeteria, or on the playing field, or on the campus during the authorized hours, he may express his opinions, even on controversial subjects like the conflict in Vietnam, if he does so without "materially and substantially interfer[ing] with the requirements of appropriate discipline in the operation of the school" and without colliding with the rights of others. But conduct by the student, in class or out of it, which for any reason—whether it stems from time, place, or type of behavior—materially disrupts classwork or involves substantial disorder or invasion of the rights of others is, of course, not immunized by the constitutional guarantee of freedom of speech.

Under our Constitution, free speech is not a right that is given only to be so circumscribed that it exists in principle but not in fact. Freedom of expression would not truly exist if the right could be exercised only in an area that a benevolent government has provided as a safe haven for crackpots. The Constitution says that Congress (and the States) may not abridge the right to free speech. This provision means what it says. We properly read it to permit reasonable regulation of speech-connected activities in carefully restricted circumstances. But we do not confine the permissible exercise of First Amendment rights to a telephone booth or the four corners of a pamphlet, or to supervised and ordained discussion in a school classroom.

If a regulation were adopted by school officials forbidding discussion of the Vietnam conflict, or the expression by any student of opposition to it anywhere on school property except as part of a prescribed classroom exercise, it would be obvious that the regulation would violate the constitutional rights of students, at least if it could not be justified by a showing that the students' activities would materially and substantially disrupt the work and discipline of the school.

These petitioners merely went about their ordained rounds in school. Their deviation consisted only in wearing on their sleeves a band of black cloth, not more than two inches wide. They wore it to exhibit their disapproval of the Vietnam hostilities and their advocacy of a truce, to make their views known, and, by their example, to influence others to adopt them. They neither interrupted school activities nor sought to intrude in the school affairs or the lives of others. They caused discussion outside of the classrooms, but no interference with work and no disorder. In the circumstances, our Constitution does not permit officials of the State to deny their form of expression.

We express no opinion as to the form of relief which should be granted, this being a matter for the lower courts to determine. We reverse and remand for further proceedings consistent with this opinion.

Mr. Justice Black, dissenting.

The Court's holding in this case ushers in what I deem to be an entirely new era in which the power to control pupils by the elected "officials of state supported public schools * * *" in the United States is in ultimate effect transferred to the Supreme Court.

Assuming that the Court is correct in holding that the conduct of wearing armbands for the purpose of conveying political ideas is protected by the First Amendment, the crucial remaining questions are whether students and teachers may use the schools at their whim as a platform for the exercise of free speech—"symbolic" or "pure"—and whether the courts will allocate to themselves the function of deciding how the pupils' school day will be spent.

While the absence of obscene remarks or boisterous and loud disorder perhaps justifies the Court's statement that the few armband students did not actually "disrupt" the classwork, I think the record overwhelmingly shows that the armbands did exactly what the elected school officials and principals foresaw they would, that is, took the students' minds off their classwork and diverted them to thoughts about the highly emotional subject of the Vietnam war. [And I repeat that] if the time has come when pupils of state-supported schoools, kindergartens, grammar schools, or high schools, can defy and flout orders of school officials to keep their minds on their own schoolwork, it is the beginning of a new revolutionary era of permissiveness in this country fostered by the judiciary.

I deny [therefore,] that it has been the "unmistakable holding of this Court for almost 50 years" that "students" and "teachers" take with them into the "schoolhouse gate" constitutional rights to "freedom of speech or expression." The truth is that a teacher of kindergarten, grammar school, or high school pupils no more carries into a school with him a complete right to freedom of speech and expression than an anti-Catholic or anti-Semite carries with him a complete freedom of speech and religion into a Catholic church or Jewish synagogue. It is a myth to say that any person has a constitutional right to say what he pleases, where he pleases, and when he pleases. Our Court has decided precisely the opposite.

In my view, teachers in state-controlled public schools are hired to teach there . . . certainly a teacher is not paid to go into school and teach subjects the State does not hire him to teach as a part of its selected curriculum. Nor are public school students sent to the schools at public expense to broadcast political or any other views to educate and inform the public. The original idea of schools, which I do not believe is yet abandoned as worthless or out of date, was that children had not yet reached the point of experience and wisdom which enabled them to teach all of their elders. It may be that the Nation has outworn the old-fashioned slogan that "children are to be seen not heard," but one may, I hope, be permitted to harbor the thought that taxpayers send children to school on the premise that at their age they need to learn, not teach.

Change has been said to be truly the law of life but sometimes the old and the tried and true are worth holding. The schools of this Nation have undoubtedly contributed to giving us tranquility and to making us a more law-abiding people. Uncontrolled and uncontrollable liberty is an enemy to domestic peace. We cannot close our eyes to the fact that some of the country's greatest problems are crimes committed by the youth, too many of school age. School discipline, like parental discipline, is an integral and important part of training our children to be good citizens—to be better citizens. Here a very small number of students have crisply and summarily refused to obey a school order designed to give pupils who want to learn the opportunity to do so. One does not need to be a prophet or the son of a prophet to know that after the Court's holding today some students in Iowa schools and indeed in all schools will be ready, able, and willing to defy their teachers on practically all orders. This is the more unfortunate for the schools since groups of students all over the land are already running loose, conducting break-ins, sit-ins, lie-ins, and smash-ins. Many of these student groups, as is all too familiar to all who read the newspapers and watch the television news programs, have already engaged in rioting, property seizures, and destruction. They have picketed schools to force students not to cross their picket lines and have too often violently attacked earnest but frightened students who wanted an education that the pickets did not want them to get. Students engaged in such activities are apparently confident that they know far more about how to operate public school systems than do their parents, teachers, and elected school officials. It is no answer to say that the particular students here have not yet reached such high points in their demands to attend classes in order to exercise their political pressures. Turned loose with lawsuits for damages and injunctions against their teachers as they are here, it is nothing but wishful thinking to imagine that young, immature students will not soon believe it is their right to control the schools rather than the right of the States that collect the taxes to hire the teachers for the benefit of the pupils. This case, therefore, wholly without constitutional reasons in my judgment, subjects all the public schools in the country to the whims and caprices of their loudest-mouthed, but maybe not their brightest, students. I, for one, am not fully persuaded that school pupils are wise enough, even with this Court's expert help from Washington, to run the 23,390 public school systems in our 50 States. I wish, therefore, wholly to disclaim any purpose on my part to hold that the Federal Constitution compels the teachers, parents, and elected school officials to surrender control of the American public school system to public school students. I dissent.

GOSS v. LOPEZ
Jan. 22, 1975

Mr. Justice White delivered the opinion of the Court.

This appeal by various administrators of the Columbus, Ohio, Public School System ("CPSS") challenges the judgment of a three-judge federal court, declaring that appellees—various high school students in the CPSS—were denied due process of law contrary to the command of the Fourteenth Amendment in that they were temporarily suspended from their high schools without a hearing either prior to suspension or within a reasonable time thereafter, and enjoining the administrators to remove all references to such suspensions from the students' records.

Two named plaintiffs, Dwight Lopez and Betty Crome, were students at the Central High School and McGuffey Junior High School, respectively. The former was suspended in connection with a disturbance in the lunchroom which involved some physical damage to school property. Lopez testified that at least 75 other students were suspended from his school on the same day. He also testified below that he was not a party to the destructive conduct but was instead an innocent bystander. Because no one from the school testified with regard to this incident, there is no evidence in the record indicating the official basis for concluding otherwise. Lopez *never had a hearing*.

Betty Crome was present at a demonstration at a high school different from the one she was attending. There she was arrested together with others, taken to the police station, and released without being formally charged. Before she went to school on the following day, she was notified that she had been suspended for a 10-day period. Because no one from the school testified with respect to this incident, the record does not disclose how the McGuffey Junior High School principal went about making the decision to suspend Betty Crome nor does it disclose on what information the decision was based. It is clear from the record that *no hearing* was ever held.

II.

At the outset, appellants contend that because there is no constitutional right to an education at public expense, the Due Process Clause does not protect against expulsions from the public school system. This position misconceives the nature of the issue and is refuted by prior decisions. The Fourteenth Amendment forbids the State to deprive any person of life, liberty or property without due process of law. Protected interests in property are normally "not created by the Constitution. Rather, they are created and their dimensions are defined" by an independent source such as state statutes or rules entitling the citizen to certain benefits. Having chosen to extend the right to an education to people of appellees' class generally, Ohio may not withdraw that right on grounds of misconduct absent fundamentally fair procedures to determine whether the misconduct has occurred. The authority possessed by the State to prescribe and enforce standards of conduct in its schools, although concededly very broad, must be exercised consistently with constitutional safeguards. Among other things, the State is constrained to recognize a student's legitimate entitlement to a public education as a property interest which is protected by the Due Process Clause and which may not be taken away for misconduct without adherence to the minimum procedures required by that clause.

The Due Process Clause also forbids arbitrary deprivations of liberty. "Where a person's good name, reputation, honor, or integrity is at stake because of what the government is doing to him," the minimal requirements of the clause must be satisfied. School authorities here suspended appellees from school for periods of up to 10 days based on charges of misconduct. If sustained and recorded, those charges could seriously damage the students' standing with their fellow pupils and their teachers as well as interfere with later opportunities for higher education and employment. It is apparent that the claimed right of the State to determine unilaterally and without process whether that misconduct has occurred immediately collides with the requirements of the Constitution.

Appellants proceed to argue that even if there is a right to a public education protected by the Due Process Clause generally, the clause comes into play only when the State subjects a student to a "severe detriment or grievous loss." The loss of 10 days, it is said, is neither severe nor grievous and the Due Process Clause is therefore of no relevance. Appellee's argument is again refuted by our prior decisions; for in determining "whether due process requirements apply in the first place, we must look not to the 'weight' but to the *nature* of the interest at stake."

A short suspension is of course a far milder deprivation than expulsion. But, "education is perhaps the most important function of state and local governments." . . . and the total exclusion from the educational process for more than a trivial period, and certainly if the suspension is for 10 days, is a serious event in the life of the suspended child. Neither the property interest in educational benefits temporarily denied nor the liberty interest in reputation, which is also implicated, is so insubstantial that suspensions may constitutionally be imposed by any procedure the school chooses, no matter how arbitrary.

III.

"Once it is determined that due process applies, the question remains what process is due." At the very minimum, therefore, students facing suspension and the consequent interference with a protected property interest must be given *some* kind of notice and afforded *some* kind of hearing. "Parties whose rights are to be affected are entitled to be heard; and in order that they may enjoy that right they must first be notified."

The student's interest is to avoid unfair or mistaken exclusion from the educational process, with all of its unfortunate consequences. The Due Process Clause will not shield him from suspensions properly imposed, but it disserves both his interest and the interest of the State if his suspension is in fact unwarranted. The concern would be mostly academic if the disciplinary process were a totally accurate, unerring process, never mistaken and never unfair. Unfortunately, that is not the case, and no one suggests that it is. Disciplinarians, although proceeding in utmost good faith, frequently act on the reports and advice of others; and the controlling facts and the nature of the conduct under challenge are often disputed. The risk of error is not at all trivial, and it should be guarded against if that may be done without prohibitive cost or interference with the educational process.

The difficulty is that our schools are vast and complex. Some modicum of discipline and order is essential if the educational function is to be per formed. Events calling for discipline are frequent occurrences and some times require immediate, effective action. Suspension is considered not only to be a necessary tool to maintain order but a valuable educational device.

The prospect of imposing elaborate hearing requirements in every suspension case is viewed with great concern, and many school authorities may well prefer the untrammeled power to act unilaterally, unhampered by rules about notice and hearing. But it would be a strange disciplinary system in an educational institution if no communication was sought by the disciplinarian with the student in an effort to inform him of his defalcation and to let him tell his side of the story in order to make sure that an injustice is not done.

We do not believe that school authorities must be totally free from notice and hearing requirements if their schools are to operate with acceptable efficiency. Students facing temporary suspension have interests qualifying for protection of the Due Process Clause, and due process requires, in connection with a suspension of 10 days or less, that the student be given oral or written notice of the charges against him and, if he denies them, an explanation of the evidence the authorities have and an opportunity to present his side of the story. The clause requires at least these rudimentary precautions against unfair or mistaken findings of misconduct and arbitrary exclusion from school.

There need be no delay between the time "notice" is given and the time of the hearing. In the great majority of cases the disciplinarian may informally discuss the alleged misconduct with the student minutes after it has occurred. We hold only that, in being given an opportunity to explain his version of the facts at this discussion, the student first be told what he is accused of doing and what the basis of the accusation is.

Since the hearing may occur almost immediately following the misconduct, it follows that as a general rule notice and hearing should precede removal of the student from school. We agree with the District Court, however, that there are recurring situations in which prior notice and hearing cannot be insisted upon. Students whose presence poses a continuing danger to persons or property or an ongoing threat of disrupting the academic process may be immediately removed from school. In such cases, the necessary notice and rudimentary hearing should follow as soon as practicable, as the District Court indicated.

In holding as we do, we do not believe that we have imposed procedures on school disciplinarians which are inappropriate in a classroom setting. Instead we have imposed requirements which are, if anything, less than a fair-minded school principal would impose upon himself in order to avoid unfair suspensions.

We stop short of construing the Due Process Clause to require, country-wide, that hearings in connection with short suspensions must afford the student the opportunity to secure counsel, to confront and cross-examine witnesses to verify his version of the incident. Brief disciplinary suspensions are almost countless. To impose in each such case even truncated trial type procedures might well overwhelm administrative facilities in many places and, by diverting resources, cost more than it would save in educational effectiveness. Moreover, further formalizing the suspension process and escalating its formality and adversary nature may not only make it too costly as a regular disciplinary tool but also destroy its effectiveness as part of the teaching process.

On the other hand, requiring effective notice and informal hearing permitting the student to give his version of the events will provide a meaningful hedge against erroneous action. At least the disciplinarian will be alerted to the existence of disputes about facts and arguments about cause and effect. He may then determine himself to summon the accuser, permit cross-examination and allow the student to present his own witnesses. In more difficult cases, he may permit counsel. In any event, his discretion will be more informed and we think the risk of error substantially reduced.

Requiring that there be at least an informal give-and-take between student and disciplinarian, preferably prior to the suspension, will add little to the fact-finding function where the disciplinarian has himself witnessed the conduct forming the basis for the charge. But things are not always as they seem to be, and the student will at least have the opportunity to characterize his conduct and put it in what he deems the proper context.

We should also make it clear that we have addressed ourselves solely to the short suspension, not exceeding 10 days. Longer suspensions or expulsions for the remainder of the school term, or permanently, may require more formal procedures. Nor do we put aside the possibility that in unusual situations, although involving only a short suspensions, something more than the rudimentary procedures will be required.

IV.

The District Court found each of the suspensions involved here to have occurred without a hearing, either before or after the suspension, and that each suspension was therefore invalid and the statute unconstitutional insofar as it permits such suspensions without notice or hearing. Accordingly, the judgment is *Affirmed.*

Mr. Justice Powell, with whom The Chief Justice, Mr. Justice Blackmun, and Mr. Justice Rehnquist join, dissenting.

The Court today invalidates an Ohio statute that permits student suspensions from school without a hearing "for not more than ten days." The decision unnecessarily opens avenues for judicial intervention in the operation of our public schools that may affect adversely the quality of education. The Court holds for the first time that the federal courts, rather than educational officials and state legislatures, have the authority to determine the rules applicable to routine classroom discipline of children and teenagers in the public schools. It justifies this unprecedented intrusion into the process of elementary and secondary education by identifying a new constitutional right: the right of a student not to be suspended for as much as a single day without notice and a due process hearing either before or promptly following the suspension.

In an age when the home and church play a diminishing role in shaping the character and value judgments of the young, a heavier responsibility falls upon the schools. When an immature student merits censure for his conduct, he is rendered a disservice if appropriate sanctions are not applied or if procedures for their application are so formalized as to invite a challenge to the teacher's authority—an invitation which rebellious or even merely spirited teenagers are likely to accept.

The lesson of discipline is not merely a matter of the student's self-interest in the shaping of his own character and personality; it provides an early understanding of the relevance to the social compact of respect for the rights of others. The classroom is the laboratory in which this lesson of life is best learned.

In assessing in consitutional terms the need to protect pupils from unfair minor discipline by school authorities, the Court ignores the commonality of interest of the State and pupils in the public school system. Rather, it thinks in traditional judicial terms of an adversary situation. To be sure, there will be the occasional pupil innocent of any rule infringement who is mistakenly suspended or whose infraction is too minor to justify suspension. But, while there is no evidence indicating the frequency of unjust suspensions, common sense suggests that they will not be numerous in relation to the total number, and that mistakes or injustices will usually be righted by informal means.

One of the more disturbing aspects of today's decision is its indiscriminate reliance upon the judiciary, and the adversary process, as the means of resolving many of the most routine problems arising in the classroom. In mandating due process procedures the Court misapprehends the reality of the normal teacher-pupil relationship. There is an ongoing relationship, one in which the teacher must occupy many roles—educator, adviser, friend and, at times, parent-substitute. It is rarely adversary in nature except with respect to the chronically disruptive or unsubordinate pupil whom the teacher must be free to discipline without frustrating formalities.

We have relied for generations upon the experience, good faith and dedication of those who staff our public schools, and the nonadversary means of airing grievances that always have been available to pupils and their parents. One would have thought before today's opinion that this informal method of resolving differences was more compatible with the interests of all concerned than resort to any constitutionalized procedure, however blandly it may be defined by the Court.

No one can foresee the ultimate frontiers of the new "thicket" the Court now enters. Today's ruling appears to sweep within the protected interest in education a multitude of discretionary decisions in the educational process. Teachers and other school authorities are required to make many decisions that may have serious consequences for the pupil. They must decide, for example, how to grade the student's work, whether a student passes or fails a course, whether he is to be promoted, whether he is required to take certain subjects, whether he may be excluded from interscholastic athletics or other extracurricular activities, whether he may be removed from one school and sent to another, whether he may be bused long distances when available schools are nearby, and whether he should be placed in a "general," "vocational," or "college-preparatory" track.

In these and many similar situations claims of impairment of one's educational entitlement identical in principle to those before the Court today can be asserted with equal or greater justification.

If, as seems apparent, the Court will now require due process procedures whenever such routine school decisions are challenged, the impact upon public education will be serious indeed. The discretion and judgment of federal courts across the land often will be substituted for that of the 50-state legislatures, the 14,000 school boards and the 2,000,000 teachers who heretofore have been responsible for the administration of the American public school system. If the Court perceives a rational and analytically sound distinction between the discretionary decision by school authorities to suspend a pupil for a brief period, and the types of discretionary school decisions described above, it would be prudent to articulate it in today's opinion. Otherwise, the federal courts should prepare themselves for a vast new role in society.

INGRAHAM v. WRIGHT

April 19, 1977

Mr. Justice Powell delivered the opinion of the Court.

This case presents questions concerning the use of corporal punishment in public schools: first, whether the paddling of students as a means of maintaining school discipline constitutes cruel and unusual punishment in violation of the Eighth Amendment; and second, to the extent that paddling is constitutionally permissible, whether the Due Process Clause of the Fourteenth Amendment requires prior notice and an opportunity to be heard.

Petitioners' evidence may be summarized briefly. In the 1970-1971 school year many of the 237 schools in Dade County used corporal punishment as a means of maintaining discipline pursuant to Florida legislation and a local school board regulation.

Petitioners focused on Drew Junior High School, the school in which both Ingraham and Andrews were enrolled in the fall of 1970. In an apparent reference to Drew, the District Court found that "[t]he instances of punishment which could be characterized as severe, accepting the students' testimony as credible, took place in one junior high school." The evidence, consisting mainly of the testimony of 16 students, suggests that the regime at Drew was exceptionally harsh. The testimony of Ingraham and Andrews, in support of their individual claims for damages, is illustrative. Because he was slow to respond to his teacher's instructions, Ingraham was subjected to more than 20 licks with a paddle while being held over a table in the principal's office. The paddling was so severe that he suffered a hematoma requiring medical attention and keeping him out of school for 11 days. Andrews was paddled several times for minor infractions. On two occasions he was struck on his arms, once depriving him of the full use of his arm for a week.

The use of corporal punishment in this country as a means of disciplining school children dates back to the colonial period. It has survived the transformation of primary and secondary education from the colonials' reliance on optional private arrangements to our present system of compulsory education and dependence on public schools. Despite the general abandonment of corporal punishment as a means of punishing criminal offenders, the practice continues to play a role in the public education of school children in most parts of the country. Professional and public opinion is sharply divided on the practice, and has been for more than a century. Yet we can discern no trend toward its elimination.

At common law a single principle has governed the use of corporal punishment since before the American Revolution: teachers may impose reasonable but not excessive force to discipline a child.

To the extent that the force is excessive or unreasonable, the educator in virtually all States is subject to possible civil and criminal liability.

All of the circumstances are to be taken into account in determining whether the punishment is reasonable in a particular case. Among the most important considerations are the seriousness of the offense, the attitude and past behavior of the child, the nature and severity of the punishment, the age and strength of the child, and the availability of less severe but equally effective means of discipline.

Of the 23 States that have addressed the problem through legislation, 21 have authorized the moderate use of corporal punishment in public schools. Of these States only a few have elaborated on the common law test of reasonableness, typically providing for approval or notification of the child's parents, or for infliction of punishment only by the principal or in the presence of an adult witness. Only two States, Massachusetts and New Jersey, have prohibited all corporal punishment in their public schools. Where the legislatures have not acted, the state courts have uniformly preserved the common law rule permitting teachers to use reasonable force in disciplining children in their charge.

Against this background of historical and contemporary approval of reasonable corporal punishment, we turn to the constitutional questions before us.

The Eighth Amendment provides, "Excessive bail shall not be required, nor excessive fines imposed, nor cruel and unusual punishments inflicted." An examination of the history of the Amendment and the decisions of this

Court construing the proscription against cruel and unusual punishment confirms that it was designed to protect those convicted of crimes. We adhere to this longstanding limitation and hold that the Eighth Amendment does not apply to the paddling of children as a means of maintaining discipline in public schools.

Petitioners acknowledge that the original design of the Cruel and Unusual Punishments Clause was to limit criminal punishment, but urge nonetheless that the prohibition should be extended to ban the paddling of school children. Observing that the Framers of the Eighth Amendment could not have envisioned our present system of public and compulsory education, with its opportunities for noncriminal punishments, petitioners contend that extension of the prohibition against cruel punishments is necessary lest we afford greater protection to criminals than to schoolchildren. It would be anomalous, they say, if schoolchildren could be beaten without constitutional redress, while hardened criminals suffering the same beatings at the hands of their jailors might have a valid claim under the Eighth Amendment. Whatever force this logic may have in the other settings, we find it an inadequate basis for wrenching the Eighth Amendment from its historical context and extending it to traditional disciplinary practices in the public schools.

The prisoner and the schoolchild stand in wholly different circumstances, separated by the harsh facts of criminal conviction and incarceration.

The schoolchild has little need for the protection of the Eighth Amendment. Though attendance may not always be voluntary, the public school remains an open institution. Except perhaps when very young, the child is not physically restrained from leaving school during school hours; and at the end of the school day, the child is invariably free to return home. Even while at school, the child brings with him the support of family and friends and is rarely apart from teachers and other pupils who may witness and protest any instances of mistreatment.

The openness of the public school and its supervision by the community afford significant safeguards against the kinds of abuses from which the Eighth Amendment protects the prisoner. In virtually every community where corporal punishment is permitted in the schools, these safeguards are reinforced by the legal constraints of the common law. Public school teachers and administrators are privileged at common law to inflict only such corporal punishment as is reasonably necessary for the proper education and discipline of the child; any punishment going beyond the privilege may result in both civil and criminal liability. As long as the schools are open to public scrutiny, there is no reason to believe that the common law constraints will not effectively remedy and deter excesses such as those alleged in this case.

We conclude that when public school teachers or administrators impose disciplinary corporal punishment, the Eighth Amendment is inapplicable. The pertinent constitutional question is whether the imposition is consonant with the requirements of due process.

In any deliberate infliction of corporal punishment on a child who is restrained for that purpose, there is some risk that the intrusion on the child's liberty will be unjustified and therefore unlawful. In these circumstances the child has a strong interest in procedural safeguards that minimize the risk of wrongful punishment and provide for the resolution of disputed questions of justification.

We turn now to a consideration of the safeguards that are available under applicable Florida law.

Florida has continued to recognize, and indeed has strengthened by statute, the common law right of a child not to be subjected to excessive corporal punishment in school. Under Florida law the teacher and principal of the school decide in the first instance whether corporal punishment is reasonably necessary under the circumstances in order to discipline a child who has misbehaved. But they must exercise prudence and restraint. For Florida has preserved the traditional judicial proceedings for determining whether the punishment was justified. If the punishment inflicted is later found to have been excessive—not reasonably believed at the time to be necessary for the child's discipline or training—the school authorities inflicting it may be held liable in damages to the child and, if malice is shown, they may be subject to criminal penalties.

Although students have testified in this case to specific instances of abuse, there is every reason to believe that such mistreatment is an aberration. The uncontradicted evidence suggests that corporal punishment in the Dade County schools was, "[w]ith the exception of a few cases, . . . unremarkable in physical severity." Moreover, because paddlings are usually inflicted in response to conduct directly observed by teachers in their presence, the risk that a child will be paddled without cause is typically insignificant. In the ordinary case, a disciplinary paddling neither threatens seriously to violate any substantive rights nor condemns the child "to suffer grievous loss of any kind."

In those cases where severe punishment is contemplated, the available civil and criminal sanctions for abuse—considered in light of the openness of the school environment—afford significant protection against unjustified corporal punishment. Teachers and school authorities are unlikely to inflict corporal punishment unnecessarily or excessively when a possible consequence of doing so is the institution of civil or criminal proceedings against them.

It still may be argued, of course, that the child's liberty interest would be better protected if the common law remedies were supplemented by the administrative safeguards of prior notice and a hearing. We have found frequently that some kind of prior hearing is necessary to guard against arbitrary impositions on interests protected by the Fourteenth Amendment. But where the State has preserved what "has always been the law of the land," the case for administrative safeguards is significantly less compelling.

"At some point the benefit of an additional safeguard to the individual affected . . . and to society in terms of increased assurance that the action is just, may be outweighed by the cost." We think that point has been reached in this case. In view of the low incidence of abuse, the openness of our schools, and the common law safeguards that already exist, the risk of error that may result in violation of a school child's substantive rights can only be regarded as minimal. Imposing additional administrative safeguards as a constitutional requirement might reduce that risk marginally, but would also entail a significant intrusion into an area of primary educational responsibility. We conclude that the Due Process Clause does not require notice and a hearing prior to the imposition of corporal punishment in the public schools, as that practice is authorized and limited by the common law.

Petitioners cannot prevail on either of the theories before us in this case. The Eighth Amendment's prohibition against cruel and unusual punishments is inapplicable to school paddlings, and the Fourteenth Amendment's requirement of procedural due process is satisfied by Florida's preservation of common law constraints and remedies. We therefore agree with the Court of Appeals that petitioners' evidence affords no basis for injunctive relief, and that petitioners cannot recover damages on the basis of any Eighth Amendment or procedural due process violation.

Mr. Justice White, with whom Mr. Justice Brennan, Mr. Justice Marshall, and Mr. Justice Stevens join, dissenting.

The Eighth Amendment places a flat prohibition against the infliction of "cruel and unusual punishments." This reflects a societal judgment that there are some punishments that are so barbaric and inhumane that we will not permit them to be imposed on anyone, no matter how opprobrious the offense. If there are some punishments that are so barbaric that they may not be imposed for the commission of crimes, designated by our social system as the most thoroughly reprehensible acts an individual can commit, then a *fortiori*, similar punishments may not be imposed on persons for less culpable acts, such as breaches of school discipline. Thus, if it is constitutionally impermissible to cut off someone's ear for the commission of murder, it must be unconstitutional to cut off a child's ear for being late to class.

No one can deny that spanking of school children is "punishment" under any reasonable reading of the word, for the similarities between spanking in public schools and other forms of punishment are too obvious to ignore.

The essence of the majority's argument is that school children do not need Eighth Amendment protection because corporal punishment is less subject to abuse in the public schools than it is in the prison system. However, it cannot be reasonably suggested that just because cruel and unusual punishments may occur less frequently under public scrutiny, they will not occur at all. The mere fact that a public flogging or a public execution would be available for all to see would not render the punishment constitutional if it were otherwise impermissible. Similarly, the majority would not suggest that a prisoner who is placed in a minimum security prison and permitted to go home to his family on the weekends should be any less entitled to Eighth Amendment protections than his counterpart in a maximum security prison. In short, if a punishment is so barbaric and inhumane that it goes beyond the tolerance of a civilized society, its openness to public scrutiny should have nothing to do with its constitutional validity.

To guard against this risk of punishing an innocent child, the Due Process Clause requires, not an "elaborate hearing" before a neutral party, but simply "an informal give-and-take between student and disciplinarian" which gives the student "an opportunity to explain his version of the facts."

The Court now holds that these "rudimentary precautions against unfair or mistaken findings of misconduct," are not required if the student is punished with "appreciable physical pain" rather than with a suspension, even though both punishments deprive the student of a constitutionally protected interest. Although the respondent school authorities provide absolutely *no* process to the student before the punishment is finally inflicted, the majority concludes that the student is nonetheless given due process because he can later sue the teacher and recover damages if the punishment was "excessive."

This tort action is utterly inadequate to protect against erroneous infliction of punishment for two reasons. First, under Florida law, a student punished for an act he did not commit cannot recover damages from a teacher "proceeding in utmost good faith . . . on the reports and advice of others"; the student has no remedy at all for punishment imposed on the basis of mistaken facts, at least as long as the punishment was reasonable from the point of view of the disciplinarian, uninformed by any prior hearing. The "traditional common law remedies" on which the majority relies, thus do nothing to protect the student from the danger that concerned the Court in *Goss*—the risk of reasonable, good faith mistake in the school disciplinary process.

Second, and more important, even if the student could sue for good faith error in the infliction of punishment, the lawsuit occurs after the punishment has been finally imposed. The infliction of physical pain is final and irreparable; it cannot be undone in a subsequent proceeding. There is every reason to require, as the Court did in *Goss*, a few minutes of "informal give-and-take between student and disciplinarian" as a "meaningful hedge" against the erroneous infliction of irreparable injury.

There is, in short, no basis in logic or authority for the majority's suggestion that an action to recover damages for excessive corporal punishment "afford[s] substantially greater protection to the child than the informal conference mandated by *Goss*." The majority purports to follow the settled principle that what process is due depends on "'the risk of an erroneous deprivation of [the protected] interest . . . and the probable value, if any, of additional or substitute procedural safeguards'"; it recognizes, as did *Goss*, the risk of error in the school disciplinary process and concedes that "the child has a strong interest in procedural safeguards that minimize the risk of wrongful punishment. . . ," but it somehow concludes that this risk is adequately reduced by a damage remedy that never has been recognized by a Florida court, that leaves unprotected the innocent student punished by mistake, and that allows the State to punish first and hear the student's version of events later. I cannot agree.

Appendix D

Statement of Policy on School Records

(The Family Educational Rights and Privacy Act)

The statement that follows is the policy of the Chattanooga Public Schools concerning school records and is made available to all parents. This policy incorporates the basic provisions of the Family Educational Rights and Privacy Act of 1974. Beyond that it reflects a sense of obligation about school records, why they are kept, and who should or should not have access to them.

There are differences in the problems different school districts face; therefore the specifics of a school records policy may vary from one place to another. But on the whole this statement represents the kind of policy on school records every school district should make public.

Student Records

Policy Statement

The Chattanooga Board of Education recognizes the obligation of the professional staff of the school district to maintain pupil records which will contribute positively to the purposes of instructional planning, accurate reporting to parents on pupil progress, and the fulfillment of accountability requirements in educational operations. In respect for the rights of pupils and parents to privacy and confidentiality with regard to the maintenance and use of educational records and all information contained in such records, the Board will comply with the requirements and intent of the Family Education Rights and Privacy Act of 1974 (Section 513 of Public Law 93.380).

A copy of the policy statement and the accompanying regulations contained in the Policy Book of the Chattanooga Public Schools may be obtained on request from the principal of any school in the system. Publication in this handbook is in compliance with requirements for annual notice to parents and adult students of specified regulations concerning student records, including the right of confidentiality, the right of access and the right of challenge of records. (See "Rights of Parents or Adult Students.")

Records Maintained

The records listed below are maintained in the school for each pupil enrolled.

Enrollment Information—Collected each school year. The principal is responsible for maintenance. Information includes student's legal name, birth data (place, date, and birth certificate number), current address, parents, and guardian, if any.

Emergency Health Information—Collected each school year. The principal is responsible for maintenance in the elementary school, and the school nurse has responsibility in secondary school. Information concerning such health conditions as diabetes, allergies, heart condition or other restricting health factors; name of family physician, and where parent or guardian may be reached in emergency.

Cumulative Record, Grades K-8—Begun when student enrolls in kindergarten or elementary school and maintained in the school for the duration of the student's enrollment in the school system. In elementary, the principal is responsible for maintenance; the guidance counselor maintains the record in secondary schools. It includes identifying information (legal name, birth data, race, sex), enrollment history, grades earned, results of standardized tests, awards earned, extra-curricular activities and interests, health records, and reports of supportive services, if any.

Cumulative Record, Grades 9-12—Begun when student enrolls in ninth grade and maintained in the school for the duration of the student's enrollment in the school system. Guidance counselor is responsible for maintenance. Information includes same type of information kept on elementary record, in addition to vocational interests and experiences, and results of college entrance examinations, if any.

Permanent Record—Maintained in the school for current information while the student is enrolled and later filed in the school for permanent reference as a service to former students. The school principal is responsible for maintenance of the record, which contains identifying information, parent identification, credits earned, grades earned, attendance information, results of college entrance examination, and special education services received, if any.

The following records are also maintained on students enrolled at the school if applicable:

Athletic Records—Maintained by the athletic director of each secondary school. They are kept for permanent reference as a service to former students, and contain information concerning height, weight, and records obtained in participation in officially recognized athletics or sports activities.

Discipline Records—Maintained during the school year for accounting purposes by the principal of each school. Information includes identifying data (student's name, race, sex), description of offense, title of person imposing disciplinary action, procedures followed before imposition of the action.

Special Education Records—Begun when student receives special education services, and maintained by the elementary school principal, or by the guidance counselor in secondary school. They accompany the student for the duration of his or her enrollment in the school system. Information includes lists of special education services received by the student, reports of tests and examinations, reports of team or committee findings and recommendations, progress reports, referral records, record reviews, and due process procedures, including result of any hearing held.

Disclosure Records—Maintained with each record, except for those classified as directory information. It includes the name and title of persons reviewing the record, date of each review, purpose of each review, and records of parental permission for dissemination.

The following records are maintained for planning, evaluation, and accounting purposes at the Central Offices of the Chattanooga Public Schools, 1161 West Fortieth Street, Chattanooga:

Special Services Reports—Maintained in the Division of Pupil Personnel. Social work reports are maintained by the social work specialist; health services reports are maintained by the health services specialist; reports of psychological testing services are maintained by the psychological specialist.

Discipline and Withdrawal Reports—Reports of suspension, expulsion, and withdrawal maintained by the Director of Testing and Pupil Services, who is also responsible for maintenance of records concerning withdrawal from school. Records of suspension include: the name and identifying data for each pupil suspended and the nature of the offense for which each suspension was imposed. Similar records are maintained for student expulsion, with inclusion of supporting data. The name of each student withdrawing from school with the reason for withdrawal is also maintained.

Standardized Test Results—Listed on individual student records kept in the school, and also maintained in printout data for each school in the office of the Director of Testing and Pupil Services. Group data are also maintained in the files of the Director of Planning and Evaluation, and used for planning, evaluation, and accountability purposes.

Procedures for Termination of Records

Enrollment and emergency health records are terminated at the close of each school year. Permanent record cards and athletic records are maintained permanently by the school as a service to former students. Results of standardized tests are maintained permanently in central files for evaluation and assessment purposes. Other records pertaining directly to individual students, including any explanations placed in the record by the parent or adult student and any records of access for each education record, are maintained for the duration of the student's enrollment in the Chattanooga Public Schools. They are destroyed when the student may no longer reasonably be expected to re-enroll in the school system. No records may be destroyed if there is an outstanding request to inspect and review them.

Rights of Parent or Adult Student

The school system considers a parent or legal guardian has authority to exercise the rights listed below and to provide consent required unless the school system has been provided with a legally binding instrument to the contrary.

Whenever a student has reached eighteen years of age, the rights and required consent are then *only* given to and required of the student. The status of the student as a dependent does not affect these rights, except that parents of a dependent student have the right of access to the records.

The rights of parents or adult students regarding those education records maintained by the school system and directly related to a student are listed below:

Upon request, the right of access to the records. Parents have the right of access to records of students over 18 years of age, if they are dependents as defined in Section 152 of the Internal Revenue Code.

The right to receive a response to reasonable requests for explanations and interpretations of record content.

In the event the parent or adult student considers a record inaccurate, misleading or in violation of the privacy or other rights of the students, the right to challenge such information and to have opportunity for hearing, should agreement not be reached with record custodians. The parent or adult student also has the right to place in the record a statement commenting on the information and or setting forth any reasons for disagreement with the decision of the school system.

The right to determine whether records may be released; written consent for such disclosure is required, except in specified instances.

If material contains information concerning more than one student, the right to inspect and review *only* that part pertaining to the student, *or* (if the information cannot be separated from that of other students) the right to be informed of the specific information contained in such material.

The right to deny release of directory information, if written notification is given to the school system.

Procedures for Access to Records

A parent or adult student who wishes to review educational records of the student must complete the Request for Review of Student Records (FERPA Form #1), obtainable upon request from the school principal. The principal will maintain the original and a copy will be given to the parent or adult student making the request.

Access must be granted by the school system within 45 days of receiving the request from the parent or adult student. If the student is a special education student, access must be granted almost immediately.

Procedures for Obtaining Copies of Records

Copies of student records are available to a parent or student upon completion of the Request for Copy of Student Records (FERPA Form #2), obtainable from the principal. The form is to be returned to the principal.

All requests for copies made by parents or adult students are honored, except in the case of reports generated by agencies or individuals external to the school system but serving in a professional capacity in the interests of the student, and which contain information of a sensitive nature, the unguarded disclosure of which might prove damaging to the student involved. In these instances, the Chattanooga Public Schools must recognize its responsibility to the best interests of the student and to the professional-client relationship. Fees for copies are listed as follows:

Permanent record, or other record maintained on card form .... $0.50 each
Cumulative record, special education record, or record of
supportive services rendered .... $1.00 each

Agencies requesting copies of records are required to comply with regulations of the Act and with the policy and administrative procedures of the Chattanooga Public Schools.

Procedures for Challenge of Records

If the parent or adult student considers information in the student's record to be inaccurate, misleading, or in violation of the privacy or other rights of the student, he or she may request amendment, deletion, or revision of the record. The school system will decide within a reasonable length of time whether the request is to be granted or denied.

If the school system denies the request for amendment, or revision of the record, it will inform the parent or adult student, and will advise him or her of the right to a hearing.

Procedures for Hearing to Challenge Records

Upon request of a parent or adult student for a hearing to challenge educational records, the school system will comply with required procedures for hearing:

The hearing will be held within a reasonable length of time after the request and the parent or adult student will be given notice of the date, place, and time a reasonable period of time in advance of the hearing.

The hearing will be conducted by an official of the school system who does not have a direct interest in the outcome of the hearing.

The parent or adult student will be given a full and fair opportunity to present relevant evidence, and may be assisted or represented by individuals of his or her choice at his or her own expense, including an attorney.

The school system will give its decision in writing within a reasonable period of time after conclusion of the hearing.

The decision of the school system shall be based solely on evidence presented at the hearing and shall include a summary of the evidence and the reasons for the decision.

If, as a result of the hearing, the school system denies the request of the parent or adult student for amendment, deletion, or revision of the record, the person making the request may place in the records a statement commenting on information in the records and/or setting forth any reasons for disagreement with the school system.

Prior Consent for Disclosure Required

The written consent of a parent or adult student must be obtained for disclosure of any personally identifiable educational record, other than directory information or in certain specified exceptions. The consent must include the following:

Signature of parent or adult student
Date of signature
Specification of records to be disclosed
Purpose or purposes for disclosure
Party or class of parties to whom disclosure is to be made.

When disclosure is to be made, as specified above, the person giving consent may, upon request, receive a copy at his or her own expense. Upon request of the parent, the student who is not adult may also receive a copy of the record at his or her expense.

Consent is not required for disclosure to a parent of a student who is a minor, or for disclosure to the student regardless of age.

Prior Consent for Disclosure not Required

Prior consent of parent or adult student for disclosure is not required in the instances described below:

Disclosure of records to other school officials, including teachers with the school system, who are determined to have legitimate educational interests. Such officials include the following:

Members of the professional staff who have responsibility for planning, evaluation and implementing programs, activities and supportive services for individual students or for groups of students,

or

members of the professional staff who are responsible for solution of problems which have impact on the ability of individual students or of groups of students to make best use of the educational offerings available.

Transfer of records upon request of other school or school system in which a student seeks to enroll. The parent or adult student, upon request, may obtain a copy of education records transferred and may have oppor tunity for hearing as described above.

If the student receives services from more than one school, disclosure of records between the schools. The parent or adult student, upon request, may obtain a copy of records transferred and may have opportunity for hearing as described above.

Disclosure to authorized representatives of local, state, or federal author ities, in connection with procedures for auditing, evaluation, and enforce ment of compliance. Unless written consent is obtained, the information is protected so that students or parents cannot be identified by anyone other than those officials. Records are destroyed when no longer needed.

Disclosure in connection with financial aid (in post secondary school) for which the student has applied.

Disclosure to state or local officials to whom information is required by law to be disclosed.

Disclosure to organizations conducting studies on behalf of the school system for specific purposes, including improvement of instruction. Studies must be conducted in a manner to assure that students or parents cannot be identified by anyone other than representatives of the organization. The information is destroyed when no longer needed.

Disclosures to accrediting organizations in order to carry out their accrediting functions.

Disclosures to parents of a dependent student as defined in Section 152 of the Internal Revenue Code of 1954.

Disclosures in compliance with judicial order or subpoena, provided that the school system makes a reasonable effort to notify the parent or adult student in advance of compliance.

Disclosure to appropriate parties in an emergency, if the information is necessary to protect the health and safety of the student or of other individ uals.

Disclosures of directory information unless the school system has re ceived written notice to the contrary from the parent or adult student.

Directory Information

While it is the practice of the school system to discourage publication and dissemination of individual school directories, certain information is classified as directory information. It includes the following:

Student's name, address, telephone number, date and place of birth, assigned grade, major field of study, participation in officially recognized activities and sports, weight and height of participants in athletic events, dates of attendance, diplomas and awards received, the most recent school attended, and similar information.

The student's address and telephone number are never disclosed except in the educational interest of the student.

Release of other directory information may be made unless the school system receives written notification from the parent or adult student that none of the directory information may be released. This notification must be made within six weeks after enrollment of the student.

Complaints

If the parent or adult student feels that the school system has failed to comply with the provisions of Section 438 of the General Education Provisions Act, as amended, he or she has the right to file written complaint at the following address:

Fair Information Practice, Department of Health, Education and Welfare; 200 Independence Avenue, S.W.; Washington, D.C. 20201.

The office will notify each party that the complaint has been received, and after investigation of the complaint, will provide written notice of its findings.

Selected Publications on Law-Related Education

The American Bar Association: The ABA's Committee on Youth Educa tion for Citizenship publishes a number of comprehensive booklets that can be obtained by writing YEFC, 1155 East 60th Street, Chicago, Illinois 60637. These include:

- *Bibliography of Law Related Curriculum Materials: Annotated* (1976, 116 pp. $1) Describes more than 1000 books and pamphlets for classroom use and teacher reference.
- *Media: An Annotated Catalogue of Law Related Audio Visual Ma terials* (1975, 79 pp. $1) Describes more than 400 films, filmstrips, and tapes for school use.
- *Gaming: An Annotated Catalogue of Law Related Games and Sim ulations* (1975, 32 pp. $1) Describes over 130 games and simulations for classroom use and teacher reference.
- *Directory of Law-Related Educational Activities* (1974, 82 pp. Free) Information on more than 250 projects throughout the country.

Curriculum Materials

Law in a Free Society (606 Wilshire Blvd., Santa Monica, CA 90401) publishes materials for both teacher training and student use on eight basic concepts: Authority, Justice, Privacy, Freedom, Responsibility, Participa tion, Diversity, and Property. For teacher training, they have published a Guide, Casebook, Curriculum (K-12) and Lesson Plans for each concept. For use in classrooms, they are developing modules on each concept which include a sound filmstrip, a student resource book, and a teaching guide.

The West Publishing Co. (170 Old Country Road, Mineola, NY 11501) has published *Street Law: A Course in Practical Law* (1975) for use in secondary schools and adult education programs. Topics covered include Criminal Law, Consumer Law, Family Law, Housing Law, Environmental Law, and Individual Rights Law.

The Constitutional Rights Foundation (6310 San Vicente Blvd., Los Angeles, CA. 90048) publishes "Bill of Rights in Action," a quarterly for students and teachers. Each issue focuses on a particular theme such as Rights of Children, Youth and the Police, or Sex and Equality and includes court decisions, cartoons, and conflicting viewpoints to stimulate discussion and analysis.

Houghton Mifflin Co. (One Beacon St., Boston, MA 02107) has published 3 supplementary texts for history and social studies courses developed by the Law in American Society Foundation: *Law in the New Land* (1972) for upper elementary grades, *Great Cases of the Supreme Court* (1971) for junior high school and *Vital Issues of the Constitution* (1971) for senior high schools. In addition, they have published a series of six paperbacks entitled *Justice in Urban America* (1974) to provide a full course in legal studies for secondary students.

Ginn and Company (191 Spring St., Lexington, MA 02173) has published a Basic Legal Concepts Curriculum which includes two sets of booklets and a teachers' guide: *Justice and Order Through Law* (Summers, Campbell & Bozzone, 1974) for junior high schools and *The American Legal System* (Summers, Campbell & Hubbard, 1974) for high school students.

INDEX

NOTES

NOTES